Henry Hyde's Moral Universe

Where More Than Time and Space are Warped

**Dennis Bernstein
& Leslie Kean**

Common Courage   Monroe, ME

Ever had that feeling of outrage combined with
a sense you don't have all the facts?

It's time to *Read & Resist!*

Library of Congress Cataloging-in-Publication Data

Bernstein, Dennis.
    Henry Hyde's moral universe : where more than time and space are
warped / Dennis Bernstein & Leslie Kean.
        p.   cm. -- (The read & resist series)
    Includes index.
    ISBN 1-56751-167-8. -- ISBN 1-56751-166-X (pbk.)
    1. Hyde, Henry J.--Ethics. 2. Political corruption--United States--
History--20th century. 3. United States--Politics and government--
1981-1989--Moral and ethical aspects. 4. United States--Politics and
government--1989- --Moral and ethical aspects. 5. Legislators--
United States Biography. 6. United States. Congress. House
Biography. I. Kean, Leslie. II. Title. III. Series.
E840.8.H96B47 1999
328.73'092--dc21   99-24681
                                              CIP

Common Courage
Box 702
Monroe, ME 04951

(207) 525-0900 fax: (207) 525-3068
orders-info@commoncouragepress.com

www.commoncouragepress.com

First Printing

Contents

Acknowledgments   iv

Introduction   1
    Henry Hyde's Legacy

Remembering Rosie   6

Sex, Lies and Truth Squads   50

A Bandit on the Bank Board   72

Man of Zeal   114
    The Rule of Law vs.
    the Rule of Henry Hyde

Henry Hyde on Drugs   156
    In Defense of Treason

Democracy by Martial Law   182
    A "Prudent Plan"

Making an About-Face   193
    From Iran-Contra to Iran-Bosnia

Pro-Death All the Way   198
    Shredding the Constitution
    and Executing the Innocent

Index   226

About the Authors   236

Acknowledgments

At the top of our list of those deserving thanks is Tim Anderson, unrelenting citizen advocate, whose commitment to the peoples' right to know is an inspiration. Also we thank Sunil Sharma for first rate research and editorial support, along with C.S. Soong, Don Cushman and Larry Everest. Special thanks also to Debbie Barragan for various actions beyond the call of duty, and to Robert Parry for much good advice and references.

We greatly appreciate the help from attorneys Rita Barker, Ellen Eggers, Richard Burr and George Kendall in deciphering the complexities of the AEDPA. We also acknowledge Norman Sommer for his helpful information and perseverance; Bud Welch, Fred Snodgrass, Micki Dickoff and Anthony Freddie for their unique contributions; Elaine Hopkins for journalistic camaraderie; and Maureen Britell, Fay Clayton, Sara Love, Catherine McGill, Vicky Saporta, Susan Hill and Frances Kissling who helped us immensely, along with researchers from the National Abortion Federation, NOW, the Alan Guttmacher Institute, and Planned Parenthood.

And last, but by no means least, we are indebted to Greg Bates at Common Courage Press for his unwavering belief in the work. We also appreciate the work of Arthur Stamoulis and Jean Hay at Common Courage Press.

And on a personal note, Dennis Bernstein thanks George and Dorothy Bernstein for making Dennis the Menace possible. And from Leslie Kean, thanks to Jerry Rosser for all his nurturing support and to Paul McKim for the inspiration of his own struggle against injustice; and thanks also to U.G. Krishnamurti for his major impact on my life over the last ten years.

Introduction

Henry Hyde's Legacy

*Based upon what we now know, do we have a duty to
look further or look away?*
                            —Henry Hyde talking about
                    President Clinton, October 6, 1998

Henry Hyde may go down in history as the most famous
moral crusader in Congress. But it would be wrong—and
dangerous—to conclude from President Clinton's survival of an impeachment run by the House Judiciary
Chairman that Henry Hyde's moral agenda has failed.

Just who is this man? From press accounts, one got the
impression Hyde was a cross between Socrates, Clarence
Darrow and Mother Teresa. As *USA Today* put it during
Clinton's impeachment trial, the courtly sage from Abe
Lincoln's home state was simply "too intellectually honest
to throw his weight around for partisan reasons."

Indeed, he staked his claim during the Senate
impeachment trial on the highest of principles. "These
are matters of justice, the justice that each of you has
taken a solemn oath to serve in this trial. Some of us
have been called Clinton-haters. I must tell you distinguished Senators, that this impeachment trial is not for
those of us from the House, a question of hating anyone.
This is not a question of who we hate, it's a question of
what we love. And among the things we love are the rule

1

of law, equal justice before the law and honor in our public life."

Whether Clinton was lying or not, Hyde's own affairs of state and his shady personal dealings belie his professed belief in the sanctity of truth and the rule of law. Taken separately, the chapters in this book reveal a new standard for hypocrisy:

- While Clinton was accused of obstructing justice, Hyde helped undermine a Contra drug investigation thereby allowing traffickers to flood the U.S. market with tons of cocaine which destroyed thousands of lives.

- While he proclaimed no man is above the law, Hyde—as a former board member of a failed Savings and Loan that was sued for gross negligence—got off scot-free while the other eleven board members were forced to cough up nearly $1 million.

- While he cried "intimidation" because Clinton employed private investigators, the House Judiciary Chairman himself financed a private investigator to surveil a private citizen who was blowing the whistle about Hyde ripping off the S&L.

- When the story broke about his extramarital affair, he cried "intimidation" once again, threatening to send the FBI after anyone who dared to speak the truth.

- While Hyde's outrage during impeachment hearings at Clinton's obfuscation is legendary, Hyde never hesitated in his crafty, spirited defense of his good friend Oliver North, who had repeatedly lied to Congress.

- While a "pro-life" zealot and a papal knight, he is also pro-death, advocating for changes in the law to expand and speed up state-sponsored killing.

- While he has sponsored anti-terrorism legislation, the violent actions of Hyde's anti-abortion "friend"—for which the friend was tried and found liable—were deemed "heroic."

But to focus on the hypocrisy is to miss the lasting impact Hyde's actions have had on the nation. As we write, on a rainy day in mid-March of 1999, two dramatic events have just occurred which few people will link to the extreme policies of Judiciary Chairman Henry Hyde. On March 13, a bomb exploded at Femcare, a women's health clinic in North Carolina that performs abortions. Fortunately, the bomb only partially exploded and no one died—which was not the case at an Alabama clinic last year when a bomb tore apart nurse Emily Lyons. Clinic bombings and other acts of violence have been emboldened by Hyde's passage of legislation denying abortion funds to poor women, his labeling of health clinics as "death camps," and his statements that abortion is analogous to the holocaust.

Also in March, a Federal class-action lawsuit was filed against the CIA and the Justice Department for their convenient, 1982 secret agreement saying the CIA did not have to report drug crimes. This illegal pact which facilitated U.S. support for the Contras paved the way for the flood of cocaine into the U.S. which caused a horrific crack epidemic. Hyde supported arming the

Contras—many of whom were drug traffickers—and helped derail a serious investigation into these traffickers which might have stopped the epidemic.

Taken together, the chapters that follow show the real danger of a crusader bent on fundamentally altering the nature of our democracy, whose work in Congress seeks to lay the cornerstones of a very different society. Consider the changes Hyde has wrought:

- Even though Hyde railed about the sanctity of upholding the Constitution, he introduced legislation so severely undermining our constitutional right to federal habeas corpus review that many innocent people are doomed to execution.

- When the Contras were singled out for human rights atrocities and their aid cut by his colleagues in Congress, Hyde supported circumventing Congress to continue aid by any means necessary.

- When Hyde's political soulmates drafted an executive branch plan to suspend the Constitution and declare martial law, he called it "prudent planning."

Henry Hyde's Moral Universe is a modest attempt to add some balance to the public record on this most influential powerbroker from Illinois, who may yet find himself compelled to explain his own violations of the public's trust.

We were disappointed that Hyde failed to respond to repeated requests for interviews to answer questions about the serious issues raised in this book. Faxes and calls to his attorneys were also not returned.

Henry Hyde's Legacy

Finally, we'd like to dedicate this book to the victims of Hyde's program of turning democracy on its head—from those who died as a result of the Hyde Amendment to those like Tom Thompson, among the first of the innocent people to be executed as a result of Hyde's crime legislation, with many more sure to follow.

Dennis Bernstein & Leslie Kean

Chapter 1

Remembering Rosie

"Mother Teresa, you have shown the world that the most intensely human compassion—a compassion which recognizes the bond of humanity that links us to the poorest of the poor—is the substance from which sanctity is forged."

—Henry Hyde, June 5, 1997
at a ceremony honoring Mother Teresa

In 1977, Rosie Jiminez was waging a long battle to lift herself and her daughter out of poverty. It was a fight she seemed destined to win. While working part-time, receiving a small monthly welfare check, and using some hard won scholarships, she was six months away from receiving her teaching credentials in special education. This would be a major turning point in the life of the twenty-seven-year-old, Mexican-American single mother.

When Rosie discovered she was pregnant, she went to see her personal physician about obtaining an abortion. Her doctor told her that the law had changed and she could no longer get Medicaid funding for the procedure. In her pocket, Rosie had a precious $700 scholarship check she had just received—her only hope for a better life. She would not have dreamed of using this money for anything except her education, even at the risk of her own health.

Remembering Rosie

Rosie felt that her only choice was to spend $130—about half the amount of a legal abortion—for a crude, illegal abortion on a backstreet of her hometown, McAllen, Texas. So she went to the run-down house of the local abortionist, Maria Pineda. The front yard was littered with old appliances and two pails overflowing with garbage, and was guarded by a chained, snarling dog. Rosie's friend Evangelina, who accompanied her to Pineda's house that day, said Rosie went into a bedroom with a double bed, a cot and a wall-hanging overhead depicting Jesus. Perhaps Rosie was able to look up into this image and receive some comfort during the ordeal. Afterwards, Evangelina said Pineda showed her a long, red plastic tube that was used on Rosie. "Maria held up a rag. The rag had blood all over it. It was an old rag. Maria said Rosie was getting it real cheap."

The next day Rosie developed severe cramps and began to bleed. She called her cousin to arrange care for her daughter at her grandmother's house. A friend rushed her to the emergency room. Rosie screamed with pain every time the car went over a bump, and when they arrived at the hospital, she was purple around her eyes and had no feeling in her legs.

Rosie had contracted Clostridium perfringens—a rare infection that comes from dirt, feces, or the inside of intestines. Only 10 percent of those infected survive. The disease destroys red blood cells and breaks down blood vessels. In Rosie's case, at the advanced stages, her body turned a greenish brown and even the capillaries in her eyes were bleeding.

Over the course of eight long days, friends and family stood helplessly by her hospital bed as the infection slowly consumed her. On October 3, Rosie died.

If it weren't for Henry Hyde's legislation known as the Hyde Amendment—which had just outlawed the payment of Medicaid funds for abortions—the four-year-old daughter Rosie Jimenez left behind in the small town of McAllen would still have a mother.

Jimenez, whose name has been heralded in the battle for women's rights, was the first woman to die as a result of Hyde's legislation. Her death marked the beginning of decades of struggle to combat the lethal affects of the Hyde Amendment, which was renewed annually as an attachment to the fiscal appropriations bill.

Ellen Frankfurt and Frances Kissling, two writers and reproductive rights activists from New York City, went to McAllen to investigate the shocking death. In collaboration with the women of McAllen that knew Rosie, they set up a sting operation without any help from law enforcement, which led to the arrest of Maria Pineda who performed Rosie's botched abortion. They spent four months investigating Rosie's death, which was detailed in Frankfurt and Kissling's 1979 book, *Rosie: The Investigation of a Wrongful Death*.

Two weeks after Rosie's death, one of the doctors who had treated her in the hospital called the Center for Disease Control (CDC) in Atlanta and reported seeing four other abortion complications, including two highly unusual ones involving tetanus. Rosie's was so far the only fatality in this cluster of five, but officials had no idea how many other women would meet a similar fate. At that point the CDC launched an investigation and sent two doctors into McAllen, Texas.

On November 4, 1977, the CDC issued its report stating that Rosie Jiminez had been informed by her physician that Medicaid no longer paid for abortions.

The report then erroneously stated that "She subsequently obtained an induced abortion in Mexico." The report did note that "This is the first confirmed illegal abortion-related death reported to the CDC since February 2, 1976...Texas withdrew financial support for abortions after federal support was withdrawn on August 4." Also in error, Rosie's personal physician stated that she would not have chosen to use Medicaid funds even if they were available. In a racist and sexist stereotyping, it was implied that like other Mexican-American women, Rosie was ashamed of her sexuality and didn't trust the Anglo health care system.

The media widely echoed these errors and stereotypes proffered by public health officials and the McAllen doctors. A *New York Times* editorial titled "First Victim" said that Rosie went to "a nearby Mexican border town" and paid forty dollars for her abortion. *The Washington Post* reported that Rosie was "trying to keep her pregnancy secret when she slipped across the border to have the operation performed in the back of a Mexican pharmacy." The point behind these errors was boldly stated up front by the *Boston Globe*: "Serious doubt has been raised about a widely reported allegation that a Mexican-American woman, who died after crossing the Texas border in September for a Mexican abortion, went there because of a cutoff in federal Medicaid funds."

Angered by these reports, Frankfort and Kissling discovered some inconvenient facts countering those bent on shielding the Hyde Amendment by pinning the cause of Rosie's death on a desire to circumvent the system. The idea that she would have been too ashamed to seek a Medicaid-funded abortion even if it had been available didn't fit with the fact that she had already had one earlier that year. Debunking another distortion, the two investigators revealed that the abortion that killed Rosie took place in the U.S., making it impossible to shift blame to practices in Mexico. Frankfort and Kissling further confirmed that she had requested Medicaid for a legal abortion from her doctor before resorting to an illegal one. As far as she was concerned, she had no choice but to go the route that took her life.

These revelations forced a second CDC investigation three months after the first, acknowledging these facts.

Rosie was not the only one to die in the immediate fallout from Hyde's legislation. An African-American woman in New York died from a self-induced abortion. She had read the news about the cutoff of federal funds and didn't realize that state funds were available to her in New York. Other injuries also resulted. A woman from South Carolina gave herself an abortion with a Drano douche. She was given a hysterectomy and almost died. Marla Pitchford of Kentucky tried to abort herself with a knitting needle. In a bizarre twist, she was turned over to police, and for a while was charged with manslaughter of the fetus.

In 1980, the Center for Disease Control reported that a thirty-seven-year-old woman in Georgia died after attempting to abort herself with a glass thermometer. This happened after she was denied a Medicaid-funded abortion, and after previous attempts at self-abortion for other pregnancies.

In Louisiana, a single mother who had just lost her job could not get Medicaid for an abortion. She died after her friend attempted an abortion with Q-Tips.

Henry Hyde is not a man easy to forget, recalls Frances Kissling, now with the group Catholics for Free

Choice. She remembers an illuminating instance during the American Public Health Association annual meeting at the time of Rosie's death. The anti-abortion caucus had invited Henry Hyde to speak. After his lecture, Kissling observed him push someone out of the way who was trying to speak to him. "There is nothing gentlemanly about Henry Hyde's history," says Kissling. "He was and is a zealot in the anti-abortion movement. He is opposed even to exceptions to the Hyde amendment for women who have been raped or are the victims of incest. He has talked about these as 'loopholes' where women will lie about their sexual history in order to get an abortion. There is not one iota of respect for women that I have ever heard come out of Henry Hyde's mouth."

Over the years, as women unknown to Henry Hyde have injured themselves and died from botched abortions, the architect of the law causing this suffering has received recognition for his crusade against abortion. Meanwhile, Rosie Jimenez is still remembered and mourned, her name coloring banners used in protests and memorials when women come together in the name of reproductive rights. "We will not tolerate the death of a single woman from a butchered abortion caused by a lack of funding," write Frankfort and Kissling at the end of their book. "For each of us the life of one woman is significant."

A Politician's Compassion for the Poor

The 1976 Hyde Amendment was the first of many actions Henry Hyde would take against women's rights. He never let his disregard for his own marital oath less than a decade earlier get in the way of his launching a congressional career which exploited family values and advocated the Catholic point of view on birth control and abortion. Yet, by denying Medicaid funding for abortions, he did not emulate the sanctity he so admired in Mother Teresa by showing compassion for the poorest of the poor. Instead, Hyde established a classist system with regard to choices in reproductive health care. To this day, wealthier women are essentially unaffected by legislation that has a devastating affect on the well being of poor women.

For each of the first three years that his annual amendment passed, the Senate attached exceptions that allowed federal funding of Medicaid abortions for pregnancies that resulted from rape or incest, and if the mother faced "severe and physical health damage" from her pregnancy. But for the next twelve years—from 1981 through 1993—pro-lifers eliminated even these exceptions, restoring the amendment to Hyde's original intent. During these years, the bill read: "None of the funds appropriated under the Act shall be used to perform abortions except where the life of the mother would be endangered if the fetus were carried to term."

In the early '80s, Native Americans, federal employees and their dependents, military personnel and their dependents, Peace Corps volunteers, and federal prisoners were added to the list of those restricted by the Hyde Amendment. Despite eventual victory by the pro-choice movement in reinstating funding of abortions in case of rape or incest a few years ago, Hyde fought the change all the way. According to Hyde, even violent rape does not justify abortion. "Rape is horrible. The only thing worse than rape is abortion. That's killing," he says.

Over the years, some Representatives have joined women throughout the country and stood up to Hyde on this issue. In one instance, Representative Cynthia A.

McKinney of Georgia incurred the wrath of the staunch anti-abortionist and he responded by questioning the motivation of those advocating for poor women. During a passionate debate in 1993, McKinney rose and denounced Hyde's ban on funding for abortions. She said that the Hyde Amendment "is nothing but a discriminatory policy against poor women who happen to be disproportionately black...and quite frankly, I have just about had it with my colleagues who vote against people of color, vote against the poor and vote against women."

Hyde responded, "We tell poor people, You can't have a job, you can't have a good education, you can't have a decent place to live...I'll tell you what we'll do, we'll give you a free abortion because there are too many of you people, and we want to kind of refine, refine the breed."

The women in the room instantly jeered Hyde and hissed. Several angrily rushed to the podium. Illinois Democrat Cardiss Collins, who is African American, shouted at Hyde, "I am offended by that kind of debate." Hyde told Collins, "I'm going to direct my friend to a few ministers who can tell her what goes on in her community."

A few weeks later, Hyde contemplated the incident in a column for the *Daily Oklahoman*, writing, "I caused a bit of a ruckus on the floor of the House of Representatives during the debate over the Hyde Amendment." In recounting the above interaction with McKinney, he seemed to take delight in the strong reaction of the women members as he described what happened. "Shouldn't we be concerned, I asked, about the ugly racial implications of Congressional support for the slaughter of unborn African-American babies? And that, as they say, hit a nerve. But it was a nerve well worth hitting." He goes on to say that "the attempt to keep 'those people' from overbreeding has long been the dirty little secret of that powerful movement."

In 1998, Hyde had the satisfaction of seeing his amendment become permanent law, when it was included in the "Fiscal Year 1997 Omnibus Appropriations Bill" and thus no longer required an annual vote for renewal. Representative Diana DeGette of Colorado had warned President Clinton about the dire consequences of the legislation, urging him not to make it permanent. "President Clinton and other pro-choice advocates must stare down this effort to create a two-tiered health care system for women," she said in 1997. "Millions of lower-income women need him to aggressively oppose these discriminatory provisions and veto any legislation that contains these noxious restrictions." Now the millions don't even get an annual review, thanks to Henry Hyde.

"Goddam Henry Hyde"

"I do not want to demean women; my God, no. I was married for forty-five years. I have had a mother, a sister, a daughter. I never would want to demean women."

—Henry Hyde, July 23, 1998

Catherine McGill works on the front lines with the victims of Hyde's cutbacks. A Canadian social worker, she is the supervisor of a nation-wide abortion hotline operated by the National Abortion Federation (NAF). The hotline receives 1,600 calls a month, about half of which are from women suffering as a direct result of Hyde's legislation. The impact of the pain she encounters daily permeates her voice with an intensity which seems to come from a combination of frustration, empathy and alarm. Lurking in the background is her fear that one day there will be so many women asking her for help that she won't be able to meet the need.

"Henry Hyde has made women's lives miserable over this issue more than any other person in the country," she says. Of all the problems that arise for poor women around abortion, their inability to pay for their abortions "is the biggest issue I deal with on a daily basis." Her wish? "I would like Henry Hyde to come back as a sixteen-year-old rape victim with no money. I would like him to meet and speak with these women," says McGill from her headquarters in Washington, DC.

According to the Alan Guttmacher Institute, approximately 20 to 35 percent of women who would have had an abortion if funding were available have been forced to bear unwanted children since the passage of the Hyde Amendment. Most of the others endured great hardship to come up with the money to get their abortions anyway. For these women living in poverty, money has to be diverted from monthly bills, such as rent or utilities, or from food and clothing for the children. Some women resort to theft or prostitution out of desperation for the cash. And it takes time to scrounge for money, pushing many abortions forward to second or even third trimester.

Making matters worse, many state Medicaid programs have taken the lead from Hyde, cutting off access to state funds. Today, only California and New York guarantee abortions to poor women. There are thirteen other states that generally fund abortions for low-income women when requested appropriately by doctors. But the rest do not. Even though states are required to fund in cases of rape, incest and life endangerment, many choose out-right not to do so. Others make assistance extremely difficult to obtain, or only fund a portion of the cost. The Hyde Amendment gives the states the message that they don't have to fund abortions, because big brother in Washington doesn't. States that are already anti-choice breathe a sigh of relief.

One recent call to Catherine McGill's hotline came from a sixteen-year-old girl in Missouri who had been gang raped. Naive and not believing she could possibly get pregnant this way, the teenager did not realize she was pregnant until quite late. Her parents are active, picketing anti-abortionists who had decried abortions even in cases of rape. She knew she could not turn to them for help. Instead, she confided in her older brother who agreed to help her. Although she was a rape victim and on Medicaid, the girl could not find an abortion provider in Missouri due to the late stage of her pregnancy. When she finally did find one, laws requiring parental consent stopped the provider from helping her. She was forced out of state. Her older brother drove for twenty-one hours straight to get her to Florida. She then needed $2,000 for her procedure, which was raised by hotline resources.

McGill also heard from a twenty-four-year-old woman who lives in a trailer in Texas with two small children. She discovered she was pregnant by a man who had disappeared from her life. Since she was in her first trimester, the cost of an abortion would not be high. But, on welfare without extra money, she was forced to start selling off her possessions—among them her television and her jewelry. Her family refused to help her, and she was forced to beg and borrow from friends. She was able to raise $150 this way, but needed $150 more. She called the hotline for help as she neared the end of her first trimester. By this time, she had exhausted all her options in dealing with the fact that Medicaid would not fund her abortion. She was almost ready to give up.

McGill picked up the case from there. "We have to tell women, what can you sell?" says McGill. "Who can you ask? Can you get ten dollars here, ten dollars there? Do you know anyone with a credit card? What about the man who got you pregnant? Have you threatened him? We go over this whole big process, asking exactly what can you scrounge together? Can you tell people it's for your rent? Can you tell people it's for your children?"

"It makes me feel sick. It makes me feel absolutely ill," says McGill. "I have to tell these impoverished women, that to get this health care that you so desperately need, you have to go out there and humiliate yourself. You have to lower yourself. You have to sell everything you own that could be possibly worth money. How easy is it to tell young children that you have to sell your television? I always tell the women you should not have to do this. Sometimes I even say 'Goddam Henry Hyde.'" In the case of the woman from Texas, NAF was able to raise the extra $150.

Another woman told McGill that she would hire herself out as an exotic dancer to help her friend raise funds for an abortion. But that was hardly the worst.

McGill recounts one disturbing conversation with a woman that she will never forget. She had gone over the whole list with her, the many questions of how and where she could raise the money. The woman was in despair. She said "I can't do this, I just can't do it." So McGill asked her, "Well, how do you want to solve this?"

She answered McGill, "Well m'am, God didn't put my body on this earth to be sold, but that's the only way I see that I'd be able to work this right now." McGill was stunned. "It sent chills down my spine," she said. "I thought, what am I telling this woman to do?" In the end, NAF was able to raise the needed funds.

"What these women are willing to do to raise this money is just beyond me," McGill says. "The desperation is unbelievable."

The Hyde Amendment not only causes financial and mental hardship, but it also threatens the physical health of many women. Sometimes a woman with health problems is in danger if she gets pregnant. Even though her doctors say abortion is a medical necessity, the woman can't get an abortion because it is not a case of life endangerment. A health threat and a doctor's decision are not enough, according to Henry Hyde.

Although the law now requires that Medicaid fund abortions for rape and incest victims, in many states there are no guarantees even for these brutalized women and girls. NAF often ends up paying for abortions that Medicaid should be covering but refuses to pay. A case in point is that of Angelina, a seventeen-year-old who was raped by a fifty-two-year-old neighbor. He threatened her so she was afraid to tell her mother. Her mother walked in on her one day when she was about to try and self abort with a coat hanger. NAF paid for her abortion. Three months later, Medicaid has still refused to provide reimbursement.

In 1997, a sixteen-year-old from Muscle Shoals, Alabama discovered she was eight weeks pregnant due to a rape. She was told through her social worker the false information that Medicaid did not cover abortions. A

NAF hotline staff member contacted three Medicaid offices in Alabama and was told by each that abortion was not allowed even in cases of rape. But when the staffer threatened to bring in a news crew from *Dateline NBC*, a Medicaid official provided procedural numbers and codes for abortion coverage—all that the girl needed to get her abortion—within twenty minutes.

Also in North Carolina, Hyde has helped create an atmosphere where the state feels justified in refusing abortions that are required by law. In late 1998, a fourteen-year-old was raped by a stranger while walking on a path near her house in the town of Forsyth. The girl—whose single mother had six kids and did not own a car or a telephone—was too frightened to tell her mother until she was several months pregnant. No provider for the child could be found in the state because North Carolina has banned abortions after the first twenty weeks. The girl, who was so small she weighed only ninety pounds, had to travel to Atlanta. The ACLU is working on a legal challenge based on this case.

Even if a person is lucky enough to get on track with Medicaid, red tape can also stand in the way. If there is incomplete documentation of a rape, or no police report within a certain time frame, that is a problem. Each state establishes its own screening and documentation procedures for rape victims. The burden of proof is on the victim and requirements can be tough.

Although rape and incest victims may be the most tragic, less than 4 percent of abortions obtained by women in this country are estimated to occur because of rape, incest or life endangerment. The vast numbers of women who suffer daily due to the Hyde Amendment still manage to get abortions because they need them.

But the cost to these women is much higher than the dollars that are so difficult to come by.

What would be the most important change if Hyde's law went off the books? According to McGill, "Women would stop having to humiliate themselves. They would not have to sell their bodies. They wouldn't have to sell their possessions. They would not have to beg from their families and friends. They wouldn't have to lie about why they needed the money. They wouldn't have to go to loan sharks and drug dealers to borrow money."

Henry Hyde is sending America's women a message. McGill picks that up from the voices and struggles she encounters every day. "Hyde is telling them that their need is not real, their need is not valid," she says. "Women know whether they can afford to raise a child, and if they can do it, they do it. If they can't they know that too, and they're not going to change their minds. So by putting them through this, Hyde is causing women to humiliate themselves. He's causing them despair, frustration and desperation."

Back to the Dark Ages: Hyde Goes Global

In 1996, Hyde co-sponsored legislation which made a drastic 35 percent cut in family planning funds going overseas—a cut of $190 million in one year—exporting his attack on women to the Third World. The impact can now be felt by women in places as far away as Bolivia, Russia, Hungary, Egypt and Uganda and in some of the world's poorest nations, such as Haiti, El Salvador and Mexico. When the bill was debated on the House floor in 1997, Hyde said "The debate isn't about family planning, it's about abortion," deflecting criticism that the cuts would eliminate access to birth control and pre-natal care.

"The campaign by abortion opponents to decimate government supported family planning services only assures that women and their families in the developing world will know more suffering and death" reads a 1996 report from five leading research organizations—The Alan Guttmacher Institute, The Futures Group, Population Action International and the Population Reference Bureau in consultation with the Population Council. Though the conclusions of the study are conservative by design, they estimate that, solely as a result of the 35 percent cut, 8,000 more women will die during pregnancy and childbirth, including deaths from unsafe abortions, and 134,000 more infants will die from a lack of postnatal care wrought by the cutbacks. Seven million couples in developing countries who would have used modern contraceptive methods will not have access to them. Four million women will experience unintended pregnancies, leading to 1.6 million more abortions. Yet Hyde focused only on the abortions rather than human lives. Sticking to his argument that an embryo is a human being, he acknowledged that abortions will moderate population gain, but only "because you are eliminating people, you're exterminating them."

The Rockefeller Foundation issued a report in 1997 that warned against the devastating affects of the U.S. abandoning its role as the leading supporter of international family planning. "At the present time, a small number of people in Congress have been able to in effect kill the program to provide assistance for family planning which has been very successful for thirty years," says the report. Rockefeller described the actions of these individuals as "very much against the best interest of the human race."

UNICEF echoes this concern, saying that improving access to family planning services is paramount to improving maternal and child health in developing countries. UNICEF reports that almost 600,000 women die during pregnancy and childbirth each year, 75,000 due to unsafe abortions or attempts at self-abortions. On a scale that overshadows the tragedy of Rosie Jimenez, Hyde's global efforts help insure that 1 million children are left motherless every year.

Even though the law prohibits the use of any U.S. funds for abortions overseas, Hyde says that family planning funds assist these groups to pay for abortions, to lobby their governments to legalize abortions, and to free up other money to promote abortions. For this reason, millions are denied access to contraception. Rep. Louise Slaughter pointed out that "this bill seeks to send our nation's foreign policy back to the dark ages of women's reproductive health…this is a matter of life and death for many women."

Hyde's argument illustrates the frightening limitations of a one-track mind. "American money should not go for killing unborn children, even if they are 'Third World' unborn children…I wish my colleagues would stop insulting our intelligence. My colleagues know and I know that if we give them a million dollars, we free up their own money for other purposes."

Hyde's own intelligence needs to be examined here, since the cutbacks on contraception and family planning that he supports actually increase the number of abortions worldwide by a factor of over a million per year. More than a fifth of the world's pregnancies end in abortion, says a 1999 report by the Alan Guttmacher Institute. Twenty-six million women have legal abortions worldwide each year and 20 million have illegal abortions. Hyde's contribution to the deaths of mothers and infants is at the same time continuing to increase, not decrease, the number of abortions undergone by women who are denied other forms of family planning.

Click Here for Censorship

Sometimes Hyde's methods of attack are forceful and up front, but at other times stealth is the chosen approach. In 1996, as part of his larger crusade against women's rights, Hyde planted a time bomb against free speech in cyberspace. By hook or by crook, even while acknowledging that the provision he wrote was unconstitutional and overzealous, Hyde dealt a blow to abortion communication on the Internet, pulling this off using an archaic, 19th century law.

Colorado Representative Patricia Schroeder called Hyde's bluff. Just one day before the final vote on the 280 page Telecom bill, she discovered, buried in the final draft, a provision authored by Hyde. "This was stealth. No one on the conference committee knew it was there," said Betty Wheeler, counsel to Schroeder and other democrats on the Judiciary Committee. Other controversial issues in the massive bill had been debated, but not this one. Schroeder discovered Hyde's decree prohibiting discussion about medicines or anything else that could be used or even intended for producing abortions "or for any indecent or immoral use."

"I was really stunned to find this," said Schroeder, who retired from Congress in early 1997. "I didn't think anyone would take something out of the retro 19th century and slap it on the Internet of the 21st century. It made no sense to me," she said in a 1999 interview.

Schroeder is referring to the archaic statute known as the Comstock law, which prohibits the mailing of indecent materials, contraceptive devices, or abortion materials. "This language in no way is intended to inhibit free speech about the topic of abortion," Hyde disingenuously claimed to the Congress. But, as it reads, his provision prohibits Internet exposure of "any drug, medicine, article, or thing designed, adapted, or intended for producing abortion, or for any indecent or immoral use; or any written or printed card, letter, circular, book, pamphlet, advertisement, or notice of any kind giving information, directly or indirectly, where, how, or of whom, or by what means any of such mentioned articles, matters, or things may be obtained or made…"

Schroeder showed no hesitation in speaking out about the abortion provision on the House floor. "What it says is absolutely devastating to women. What we are going to do is put on a high-technology gag rule with criminal penalties." John Conyers, ranking member of the Judiciary Committee, echoed her concern. "Who knew that that noxious abortion portion was in the conference report? Nobody, until it was found out about last night." These protests seemed to land on deaf ears.

"Not all the members even had a printed copy of the whole bill. This meant that people weren't players. To be a player you have to have copies of the text," said Schroeder from her office at the Association of American Publishers, where she is President and CEO. "There was no debate and I don't think anybody in the place knew it was there."

That night, Schroeder and Hyde ended up in the same conference committee meeting, where Schroeder says there was a "huge fight" over the issue of Hyde's cyber war against abortion. Hyde admitted he had over-stepped himself on this one. "My frustration was that when I asked him about it, he agreed. He'd say, oh, he didn't mean it to go that far, oh, oh, oh. He'd say it was overzealous staff, and he was surprised too, and he didn't intend it to go that far. Except we couldn't get him to undo it. My response was, OK let's quick fix it, but it never happened." Counsel Betty Wheeler said that during that meeting, "Hyde said 'everyone knows that that provision is clearly unconstitutional.' I watched that exchange—it was clear that he was sincere." His recognition of his own violation of the constitution, sincere or not, did not seem to sway the outcome of his actions.

Two months earlier, the American Civil Liberties Union had written a letter to Congress warning members of the unconstitutionality of related provisions by Hyde imposing censorship on the Internet to protect children from "indecent" speech. The letter from Laura W. Murphy, Director of the Washington National Office and Donald Haines, Legislative Counsel, said that Hyde was attempting to pass amendments to the Telecom bill that involved "schemes to impose a complex regulatory system on cyberspace information content and transmission. The Hyde proposal is unconstitutional because it takes indecency, a type of speech protected by the First Amendment, and tries to regulate it in a way that violates what the Supreme Court has said must be the touchstone for regulating protected speech."

The ACLU points out that Hyde's proposed legislation makes the Department of Justice, instead of the

FCC, in effect the regulatory agency for speech in cyberspace. "The Hyde proposal is also bad public policy because it subjects all Americans to the most narrow of community standards found in the most socially limiting of locations. Even those who have chosen to adopt the social mores of such locations would not insist on imposing those mores on the millions of Americans who have chosen to live elsewhere," says the letter.

Pat Schroeder got up the morning after her conference committee meeting with Hyde to discover that after making his clarifying statement for the Congressional Record the day before, Hyde had added a written statement to the record that backed away from the promises he made on the floor. In his usual style, this statement was slipped in surreptitiously. The statement said that online discussions about abortion were permissible, but "this statutory language is confined to those commercial activities already covered." His new emphasis on "commercial activities" means that organizations could not even list a directory of providers on a website or post medical journal articles dealing with abortion technique. Judiciary Committee counsel Alan Coffey explained that he thought this change was due to "bad staff work."

On February 8, 1996, Clinton signed the Telecom bill into law, Hyde's provision intact. President Clinton said that the "abortion provisions in current law are unconstitutional and will not be enforced." Attorney General Janet Reno followed suit by promising never to enforce Hyde's abortion restriction. In her letter to Clinton and Gore, she said that "at this early stage of litigation, no irreparable harm will befall." But as the ACLU points out, Reno's letter is not legally binding.

Prohibiting communication on abortion is unconstitutional as long as Roe vs. Wade establishes the legality of abortion. But Hyde has long sought to overturn that landmark Supreme Court ruling, and perhaps he is preparing for the future. Should he and his allies ever succeed in outlawing abortion altogether, Hyde's amendment could be used to prosecute anyone who reveals abortion information. The bill imposes penalties up to a $250,000 fine and/or five years in prison for using interactive computer services to provide or receive information about abortion.

Many, including Schroeder, think that Hyde's provision could be dangerous, and that it's just a matter of time before someone puts it to use. "Somebody with political ambitions might not care if they could win it or not," Schroeder said. "They would be carrying the mantle against abortion on the Internet. I think anything can happen in this day and age."

Many are worried about future administrations. For that reason, the ACLU, the National Abortion and Reproductive Rights Action League (NARAL), the Center for Reproductive Law and Policy (CRLP) and seventeen other groups filed lawsuits the same day that Clinton signed the bill. The groups were seeking a temporary restraining order against enforcement of Hyde's abortion provision. Federal Judge Ronald Buckwalter ruled on February 15, 1996, that the "indecency" proposals were unconstitutional, but he would not issue the restraining order, citing Reno's letter as protection enough.

Patricia Schroeder did not agree with the Judge that the necessary restrictions on enforcement were in place. She introduced legislation to delete the ban on abortion-related speech. In a "Dear Colleague" letter sent to fellow members of the House, titled "Zap the Comstock Law Before It Becomes a Computer Virus on the Internet," Schroeder asked her colleagues, "When you voted on the telecommunications bill…did you intend to criminalize speech about abortion on the Internet? Of course not!" Obviously, she was not addressing this question to Henry Hyde. Her appeal did not pass, and now we ride into the twenty-first century with the virus of Hyde's shadow looming over the computer waves.

Joseph Scheidler: A True Friend

"The rule of law is the safeguard of our liberties. The rule of law is what allows us to live our freedom in ways that honor the freedom of others while strengthening the common good."
—Henry Hyde, January 16, 1999 during
the impeachment trial of President Clinton

The stories of women humiliated, injured, and in some cases killed by Hyde's amendment are innumerable. And his attempt to undermine free speech—even while acknowledging that such speech is constitutionally protected—puts an interesting spin on his oath of office to defend the constitution. But it is his court testimony in the spring of 1998 on behalf of Joseph Scheidler, a man found liable of masterminding numerous violent attacks against women and health clinics, which reveals the stark fanaticism underlying Hyde's agenda.

Back in 1980, Scheidler founded the nationwide coalition Pro-Life Action Network (PLAN) for the purpose of organizing yearly anti-abortion meetings. He publicly launched Randall Terry's Operation Rescue at a conference in Atlanta seven years later. PLAN calls its members to regular, nationwide "conventions" where it adopts agendas of illegal conduct and sends PLAN's members to carry them out. At the conventions, they agree to new tactics, like barricading clinics with Kryptonite locks, blockading clinic doors with junker cars, and dismantling medical equipment. Scheidler himself described his activist group as the "pro-life mafia." He since founded the Pro-Life Action League, which is the organization he runs today.

On a television program in 1984, Scheidler did not hide the fact that his goal is to cause women medical complications because of the stress and fear they experience when encountering aggressive demonstrators at clinics. He said these problems increase by 8 percent when the women are harassed, declaring that "we're being effective in disturbing the doctor, the counselors, the women going in..."

Scheidler is the author of *Closed: 99 Ways to Stop Abortion*. In it, he advocates ninety-nine stunts to harass abortion practitioners and women seeking abortions, including the tracking of women entering abortion clinics through their license plates and/or private detectives, leaving violent messages on clinic answering machines, infiltrating pro-choice groups, clinic blockades, and harassing landlords and insurance companies that insure clinics. He warns his readers that they might be arrested for the methods recommended in the book. In the chapter titled "Use Inflammatory Rhetoric," Scheidler preaches that America's abortion culture must be called "holocaust" and that abortion clinics should be called "death camps." Henry Hyde has used these very words himself on many occasions, including the day he came to Scheidler's trial.

Although the book professes an opposition to violence, Scheidler's rhetoric and actions appear to contradict that message. He has vowed to stop abortion by "any means necessary." He has publicly praised convicted arsonists for their effectiveness and their zeal. In 1985, in the midst of a rash of clinic arsons and bombings, PLAN proclaimed "a year of pain and fear" for anyone seeking or providing an abortion.

Letters written by Scheidler were introduced as plaintiffs' exhibits in the trial. In one 1986 letter, Scheidler discussed the fact that he had been criticized for not condemning clinic bombings. He says that an abortion facility has "no moral right to exist...How it ceases to function is not as important as the fact that it has ceased. Therefore I am indifferent to the means. The loss of 'real estate' is trivial compared to the loss of lives in that real estate." He says he is "not into using 'violence'" and believes in non-violence. But bombing clinics is not violence, in his view: "I hardly think it is violence, since it is against brick and glass and not people." While acknowledging the positive results of clinics being closed down, he says "the list of good results that has come from the violence is clear."

Some of Scheidler's correspondence illustrates the role he played in influencing or supporting those involved in bombings, and the delight he took in the destruction. One letter tells a friend, "Thanks so much for sending the photographs of our gang in front of the bombed out abortuary—great scene." Scheidler signs the letter "Respectfully in Life." Another is written to him and says, "Here, much belated, are the pictures I took of you in front of the freshly guffed clinic in Rockville."

Scheidler justifies violence on ideological grounds. "While we disagree with burning down abortion clinics, we see that destruction as trivial as compared with the human destruction that goes on routinely inside these places," he says. "I do understand, however, the emotions that might prompt one to violence in an effort to end a greater violence." Scheidler was asked by ABC *Nightline* host, Ted Koppel, "Mr. Scheidler, you are not prepared to go along with the law of the land on this, are you?" His response was, "No, never."

This is the same man who, in a February, 1999 interview from his headquarters in Chicago, spoke fondly of Hyde as "our politician" and "a great spokesman for the movement" beginning with his authorship of the Hyde Amendment. "Henry and I have known each other for years. At my trial, he was very firm in his support of me and what I do," he said.

If Henry Hyde were to pick up the phone and dial Scheidler's Pro-Life Action League telephone hotline, he could be entertained by a scathing view of his favorite president, which likely echoes his own. On the January 26, 1999 hotline message, Scheidler calls the first lady "Hillary Road-kill Clinton" for pledging $5 million dollars to, in his words, "protect baby-killing plants." He says that President Clinton is "seeking money to secure and care for the death camps," comparing this to Hitler's financing of the death camps in the 1940s. "If Hitler financed that holocaust, it's only proper that our own Hitler, Bill Clinton, is financing this holocaust," he says.

Heroic Lawbreaking

The man Hyde would travel to Chicago to support is more than an ardent ideologue. A terrifying assault on a Florida abortion clinic in March, 1986 prompted the National Organization for Women (NOW) to file a lawsuit against Scheidler, his Pro-Life Action Network, Operation Rescue, and others. Scheidler was on the scene at the time and was one of the organizers of the attack.

Scheidler and other anti-abortion leaders, including Joan Andrews and John Burt, had traveled to Pensacola, Florida, to prepare for the attack. On the evening of March 25, Scheidler and others discussed how they would operate at the planned clinic protest the next day. Several agreed to invade the clinic the next morning. Scheidler said that he might also enter the clinic if he thought he could do so without being arrested.

According to testimony, Scheidler's gang of activists threw the clinic's administrator down a flight of stairs, seriously injuring her. A woman from NOW was shoved up against a wall, resulting in a permanent injury. The activists also damaged the clinic's medical equipment which effectively shut the clinic down for days. While others were busy wreaking havoc inside the clinic, Scheidler was outside handling press relations for his group. At the same time, he took credit for the invasion and property destruction.

While criminal charges could be filed against the activists who violently entered the clinic, the only law on the books at the time that could be used against Scheidler himself for organizing the action was the federal Racketeer Influenced and Corrupt Organizations (RICO) Act. The RICO Act was established in the

1970s to prosecute profit-making enterprises such as the Mafia.

Although Scheidler was tried under RICO, Mr. Scheidler's foot soldiers had clearly violated the Freedom of Access to Clinic Entrances Act or FACE. However, this law did not come on the books until 1994. The law prohibits the use of force, threats, physical obstruction, intimidation, attempted injury or intentional injury of anyone obtaining or providing reproductive health services. It also prohibits the damaging of abortion facilities. The limitation of FACE is that it does not reach those who fund and organize the attacks on clinics and women, but is only applicable to those who actually carry out the illegal activities. This explains the need to employ RICO to reach the higher echelons of the anti-abortion hierarchy—the "pro-life Mafia"—and hold them accountable for the acts carried out by their subordinates.

In the March 1998 trial, NOW presented a compelling case that Scheidler and other abortion opponents violated the anti-racketeering laws by using violence, intimidation and extortion to stop abortion. Lead attorney Fay Clayton had deposed Scheidler eight times during the twelve years she worked on the case before the trial, and had sat across a conference table from him a number of times. "He's a very large man, overweight. He wears a hat and carries a bullhorn. He likes to tower over women. He has the demeanor of thuggery," she said.

Clayton was verbally attacked by Scheidler during the trial. According to Clayton, he put her description and that of her car on his hotline, published a picture of her in his newsletter with ugly language, and called her names. "It was very third grade kind of stuff," she says. "He's very immature and rude." Clayton says she and her family had to take security precautions, as did her firm. "He was watching us and he was not far away."

Hero Worship

Henry Hyde will go down in history as a relentless, if self-proclaimed reluctant, prosecutor of presidential perjury. Hyde's reaction to President Clinton's alleged perjury and subornation of perjury was the pinnacle of a unique brand of genteel outrage. But not a year earlier, Joseph Scheidler himself had attempted to bring in a witness for the purpose of having her commit perjury. Whether the Judiciary Chairman was aware of this attempted subornation of perjury by his friend has not been determined. In an affidavit which Scheidler signed "under penalty of perjury," he tried to persuade the court to allow Joan Andrews Bell, who was in jail at the time for violent anti-abortion activities, to testify through a deposition on his behalf. He writes in his affidavit, "Mrs. Bell told me she would testify that I had no knowledge that she or anybody else with her would enter the Pensacola clinic." In fact, Scheidler had himself stated earlier, in a written "privileged communication" to four attorneys, that there had been discussion the night before the attack on Pensacola about the possibility of entry into the clinic—either by a group of four to eight or possibly by Scheidler himself.

The judge did not allow Mrs. Bell to testify. Said Sara Love, another attorney on the case, "Scheidler is attempting to bring somebody in to lie on his behalf. And he knows it's a lie. His lawyer argued quite strongly for Joan Andrews to come in. Yet Henry Hyde came in and testified that Joe Scheidler was honest."

Prior to Hyde's arrival at the trial, dozens of patients and staff from clinics across the country spoke about Scheidler's acts of terror. Witness "Mrs. A" testified that aggressive demonstrators denied her access to a clinic in Kansas City when she approached it for her appointment for a late-term abortion. She and her husband, a naval commander, sought to terminate her pregnancy because doctors had determined that their baby would be born with only half a heart, live a very painful life and die shortly after birth. Volunteers had arranged for a special car to transport all the days' patients to their appointments in an attempt to simply get the patients into the building and away from the demonstrators. Several other women—including a fourteen-year-old rape survivor trying to terminate the pregnancy caused by the rape—were in the car with Mrs. A. These patients were physically prevented from entering the clinic on three separate days. Scheidler was in the shouting crowd that blocked them out. The doctor at this clinic was later shot.

Kathy Connor, administrator of the Delaware Women's Health Organization, testified about her moment of terror in a showdown with Joseph Scheidler. Late one Friday afternoon, when she was alone in the clinic, Connor heard the clinic bell ring and heavy footsteps coming up the stairs. Scheidler arrived with two other men, and told her, "I'm here to case the joint." She was frightened because of his reputation. She told him to leave. He would not. He put all the phone lines on hold so no one could call in. She felt trapped. Scheidler began talking to her about Catholicism and the church's stand on abortion. Connor called Susan Hill who was out of state. "She was so afraid that she didn't even do what you would normally do—call the authorities," says Hill.

When Connor finally got the police on the line, Scheidler and his accomplices left. Connor then called Hill back and stayed on the line with her until the police arrived.

The next day Hill flew into town and Scheidler was arrested for the incident. Following a "pro-life" demonstration outside the clinic, the police escorted Kathy Connor home to assure her safety. Her two small children were waiting for her there with a babysitter. As she drove up, she was suddenly shocked to see Scheidler and the two men in front of her house. She was stunned, as she had not thought to warn her children. Connor cried as she gave this testimony later. She was terrified that Scheidler knew where she lived, and terrified for her kids. Connor ended up quitting her job because the anti-abortion activities advocated by Scheidler escalated at her clinic and she was afraid for her children's safety.

This was the man Henry Hyde unabashedly called his friend and hero when he testified as a character witness during Scheidler's trial. When Hyde showed up during the fifth week, the courtroom was full, and the atmosphere was one of pomp and circumstance—at least where he was concerned. He didn't hesitate to play politics with the law, turning a serious trial into a campaign stop as he breezed through with an entourage, camera lights and media microphones. In the court lobby, he held a press conference. "Ignoring the fact that his buddy Scheidler was terrorizing women and encouraging the bombing of clinics," Clayton said, Hyde held forth about abortion as holocaust.

When Hyde marched onto the witness stand, he testified that he had known Scheidler for twenty-five years. He vouched for Scheidler's truthfulness, integrity and excellent reputation, saying that Scheidler was a friend that he saw two or three times a month and that they had "talked at some length sometimes." Hyde said, "I've never known him to lie."

It looked at the start of the day to be a triumphant turning point for Scheidler. But under the cross-examination of Lowell Sachnoff, attorney for the plaintiffs, Hyde's persona as the prima donna began to melt. Having testified that he never knew Scheidler to lie, he was asked to therefore vouch for statements Scheidler had made of illegal activities and association with convicted abortion terrorists. "If he said it, it's true," Hyde responded, taken aback.

"At the beginning he seemed like he thought he was at a political rally, trying to sell the courtroom. He could have been campaigning for himself or anyone else," said Susan Hill, president of the National Women's Health Organization who witnessed Hyde's testimony. "But after a while, he was thrown off his game. He seemed almost nervous. He was not in control of anything. To me, that was amazing—the head of the Judiciary Committee before a jury. For once, he was on the hot seat, the place he had put so many other people."

When asked if he wholeheartedly supported Scheidler in his anti-abortion movement, Hyde went all out. "He is a hero to me," he testified. "He has the guts that I wish more of us had." Sachnoff asked Hyde, "If you knew that Mr. Scheidler was advocating breaking the law, you probably wouldn't want to have anything to do with him, would you, sir?" Hyde answered, "I can't conceive of a circumstance where I wouldn't want to have anything to do with Joe Scheidler."

Sachnoff and the other lawyers for NOW geared up for attack. At one point, Hyde had stated that he believed that physically obstructing a clinic is wrong and that it should be punished, because this would be breaking the law. When confronted with the fact that Scheidler advocates physically obstructing clinic doors to prevent women from entering, Hyde claimed he was not aware of that. When confronted with a section from Scheidler's 99 *Ways to Stop Abortion*, advocating the placing of a Kryptonite lock around a person's neck and tying him or herself to a cement block in front of a clinic door, Hyde said he had not read the book. Hyde was then shown a picture of Scheidler himself blocking a clinic door, next to someone chained with a Kryptonite lock.

At this point Scheidler's counsel, Tom Brejcha, jumped in and objected. At the attorneys' sidebar that followed, the judge told Brejcha regarding Hyde, "He did it, he put his foot in it. And you are going to have to live with it."

Since Hyde had described Scheidler as "a man of strong core beliefs, a man of deep principle," Brejcha asked him on cross examination how Hyde could square his opinion on Scheidler's integrity with the fact that Scheidler was accused of advocating breaking the law. Hyde answered, "There are some people with more courage than others. Had people feeling as does Mr. Scheidler surrounded and even obstructed the entrance to Dachau or Auschwitz, there may have been fewer people incinerated there."

When Brejcha finished his brief questioning of Hyde, Sachnoff had another chance, and he moved in for the kill. It was to be the pivotal moment of Hyde's testimony. "Would you vouch for the character or the integrity of anyone who openly proclaimed that he would not obey the laws of the land?" asked Sachnoff. "Absolutely. Absolutely," Hyde enthused. "If the law of the land is immoral and condones the killing of unborn children, I think that's heroic."

Here was the Chairman of the House Judiciary Committee advocating law-breaking in front of the jury and spectators in the courtroom. "I wish you could have seen some of the jurors faces while Hyde was testifying," said Clayton later. "They knew it was politicking. They knew he was the worst kind of Congressman. Looking at the jurors, we could tell his testimony had backfired badly. They scrunched up their faces. They did not like this man. Here he was analogizing medical clinics—that give pap smears and advise women on contraception and give mammograms—calling them a death camp? That just isn't accurate."

Susan Hill, who herself testified for four straight days about abusive actions at the many clinics she oversees, is taken aback by Henry Hyde's hypocrisy, especially given his position as chief prosecutor against the President. "I thought it was amazing that, with all his speeches about the rule of law and truthfulness, Henry Hyde would give a character reference for a racketeer," she said from her office at the Raleigh Women's Health Organization in North Carolina. "He's worried about the rule of law? I find it bizarre."

But Scheidler explains it this way. "He's not talking about breaking the law by doing something immoral. If the law is immoral, you're obligated to break it. You're obligated at least not to keep it." Even though Scheidler's point makes sense to anyone trying to make change in society, he seemed to have missed the inherent contradiction of Hyde's testimony. Scheidler described it as "strong and unyielding" on his behalf, adding, "It was a sort of elation because he was so good. It was very encouraging and reassuring to hear Henry Hyde say that I was his hero."

Scheidler was not the only one to miss what had hit the jurors between the eyes. After Hyde finished and stepped down from the stand, a section of spectators wearing pro-life tee shirts staged an eruption of applause, standing up in the courtroom to cheer their man. "The jury was not impressed by that. This is a solemn proceeding; it's a trial. It is not a circus. It was offensive and very inappropriate," says Clayton.

On April 20, 1998, the women represented in the class action suit against Scheidler scored a landmark victory when a federal jury ruled unanimously that Scheidler et al. had violated the RICO act and were responsible for 121 acts including extortion, conspiracy and threats of physical violence. The penalty will be payment of triple damages.

But as of this writing, the judge has still not ruled on the injunction for the case, which will set specific limits on Scheidler's behavior. Attorney Clayton says this delay on the injunction is not surprising given the unusual nature of this case and the fact that she believes the judge is taking his time to do his best job. Because of this delay, Scheidler says he remains unaffected. "I haven't done anything different as a result of the trial," he said. "It's just the same as it was."

Clayton has a different perception. "The verdict is without question having an enormous impact," she said in a March interview. "I've heard from a lot of people at clinics who say it's been so much quieter, there's less activity. Remember, Scheidler was the leader of a whole nationwide organization, and they [the pro-life activists] were all associated with him. At the very least, they attended his annual conventions. I think they're running scared. And we haven't seen anyone step in and take his place."

Hyde's association with Scheidler also seems to have remained unaffected by his friend's new status since the trial. On October 2, Hyde was awarded the Gratiam Dei award from the American Catholic Press for his decades of anti-abortion work. It was presented at a country club in Flossmore, Illinois for $100 a plate. Hyde traveled from Washington to attend the event, and be with what he called the "heart and soul of the pro-life movement." A featured guest, along with the Archbishop of Chicago and the Greek Orthodox Bishop of Chicago, was none other than Joseph Scheidler. He stood up and read a letter he had written in praise of Hyde in which he described Hyde's outstanding performance at his trial. "He put his own reputation on the line as he took the witness stand to testify as to my reputation for truth and honesty," he read from his letter. Because of his leadership in the House on pro-life issues, "he is my hero," said Scheidler.

Speaking Truth to Power: Two Women Take on Hyde

"The abortion issue is about whether America is to be a country obsessively concentrated on rights and laws, or a country committed to a certain notion of rights and wrongs."

—Henry Hyde, 1993

Hyde did not take the women's victory in the trial easily. Three months after the guilty verdict was cast by a unanimous jury, Henry Hyde held hearings at the House Judiciary Committee at which he attempted to change the RICO law to such an extent that Scheidler's verdict could have been overturned in an appeal. He was not successful, due in large part to the courageous testimony of one woman, Emily Lyons.

Lyons is a nurse, wife and the mother of two teenage girls. She had spent twenty years working in labor and delivery and home health care for the elderly, and when she moved to Birmingham, Alabama, she went to work at a women's health clinic. On January 29, 1998, she stood fifteen feet away from a bomb that exploded outside the clinic, planted by a "pro-life" terrorist. A police officer providing security at the clinic was killed, and Lyons nearly lost her life. In the six months following the blast, she had nine operations but still dozens of pieces of shrapnel remained in her body. To this day, the nails lodged inside her knees attract magnets.

In her testimony on July 17, 1998 at Hyde's hearings on RICO, Lyons described her injuries. "My left eye was destroyed and had to be removed. My right eye was badly damaged. My right hand was mangled beyond repair. The skin was torn off my legs and my leg shattered. The blast tore a hole in my abdomen so that about ten inches of my intestines had to be removed. My eardrum was ruptured and required extensive surgery. As a result, I am now a nurse who is unable to read, write or stand for long periods of time."

Leaders of the National Abortion Federation (NAF) knew that Lyons would be the perfect witness to speak on RICO because she had experienced first hand the

Courtesy of the Southern Poverty Law Center. Used by Permission.

Hyde's brand of free speech—exclude the most powerful
Emily Lyons with her husband Jeff, taken at the time Hyde
tried to prevent her from testifying at his hearing on RICO—
where she triumphed. A nurse at a women's health clinic,
Lyons was torn apart and nearly killed by a "pro-life" bomb.

violence of anti-abortion terrorism. When Hyde heard that Maureen Britell, Director of Government Relations at NAF, was bringing Lyons in, he had the nerve to bar her from testifying. On what grounds? "Because he's Henry Hyde," said Britell. She was taken aback. Her colleague, Vicky Saporta, Executive Director of NAF, who also hosted Lyons, said that Hyde "told media and staff on the hill that he wouldn't be able to accomplish what he wanted to accomplish in the hearings if Emily were allowed to testify."

It seems obvious that the conservative Mr. Hyde does not relish dealing with strong and powerful women, particularly those whose truth overpowers his own. In his 1993 essay, "Their Dirty Little Secret," he expresses his discomfort with feminine autonomy. "A certain concept of a woman's 'autonomy,' informed by some of the more radical versions of feminist ideology, plays a dominant role in pro-abortion activism today—and has even shaped the jurisprudence of several Justices of the Supreme Court," he bemoans. Perhaps this perceived threat is what fuels his reactionary efforts to control a woman's most personal decisions. He even opposes contraception (it is "morally wrong") which, of course, could prevent abortions. Emily Lyons and Maureen Britell unleashed their autonomy on Henry Hyde, and changed history.

As Britell pointed out, responding to Hyde's refusal to let Lyons testify, "That's just not done. You don't just bar witnesses. It's never done. None of us could ever recall somebody barring a witness." Britell realized that Lyons was "a walking, living, breathing testament to the violence that the Scheidler people create. When I heard that he barred her, I said, 'That's really nice. Now I'm going to eat him alive,'" says Britell.

And she did. Britell went to the press and told them, "Guess what, Henry Hyde has just barred from testifying a woman who was just blown up." And Lyons went to extreme difficulty to come anyway. For security reasons, the police brought Britell and others out to the airport in a special bus to assist in removing Lyons from the plane prior to its being parked at the gate. The press swarmed Lyons when she arrived at the airport. She appeared on *Larry King Live* and major news shows. And she made a point to discuss Hyde's refusal to allow her testimony.

"The night before the hearing, I got a call at 7:30 saying that Henry Hyde caved. He was going to let her testify," said Britell. She and Saporta had scheduled a press conference with Lyons the next day, just before the hearing where she was going to present her barred testimony to the press and the public. "The night before, Hyde said fine, she can testify, but no press conference. Of course our response was, no deal. We're having the press conference *and* we're testifying," said Britell.

As Lyons and her entourage came into the hearing room the next day, everyone there stopped what they were doing. "You can't help but gasp when you see Emily," said Britell. "We won hands down." Congressional Representatives were reportedly ashen. All except Henry Hyde—because he didn't even show up.

During her testimony, Emily got up to show and describe each of her injuries to the committee. "Yes, there are criminal laws to deal with anti-choice extremists. However, you need only look at me to see that those laws are not enough. How could you take away a law that

45

would help prevent this from happening to someone else in the future?"

Perhaps Hyde was relieved to not have to deal with one of the most moving testimonies ever presented. "I have never seen a more emotional reaction to a witness," said Saporta "There were lots of press there. People who were listening were in tears." When they came back to vote after the break, only one Republican even returned to the room. "The testimony was so powerful they didn't even know how to deal with it," said Saporta.

Hyde's proposed amendment to RICO, designed to liberate Scheidler, never saw the light of day. "And that's precisely the reason Representative Hyde wanted to bar Emily from testifying," Saporta said. "And she did it. She stopped that legislation dead in it's tracks."

Joseph Scheidler expressed his own outrage about the powerful Emily Lyons six months after the RICO hearings. He railed at a front page *Chicago Tribune* story about Lyons which ran on January 29, 1999, the first anniversary of the bomb that mangled her. In early February, Scheidler ran a two day message about Lyons on his recorded "pro-life action news" telephone hotline. Calling her a "baby-killer" who is going around "stumping for abortion," he wondered "how many babies died in this [abortion] mill during her four years working there."

On the hotline, Scheidler also referred back to the RICO hearings six months earlier, and gives his analysis of what happened when Lyons testified. "She effectively conned some Congressmen into believing that somehow tough civil RICO laws will help keep nurses from getting shot full of nails. Fanciful and false as her testimony was, it touched the hearts of some not-too-bright Congressmen and effectively halted the hearings...the people who are leading Emily around by the nose were able, through an emotional trick, to scare the Congressmen away from much-needed RICO reform." Like his pal Hyde, he shows no respect for Lyons. He points out that she and Officer Robert Sanderson, the police officer killed by the bomb, "could be enjoying life right now if they had not been involved in the baby killing business at the new woman, all woman death camp."

As for Hyde's absence at the hearing, Vicky Saporta says she has seen Hyde walk out of the room at other hearings when women have shared their personal experiences about abortion. "He doesn't want to hear from people who have experienced violence and see the impact it has had on them," she says.

Is Henry Hyde for Real?

But on occasion Henry Hyde has managed to stick it out for painful testimony by women. Maureen Britell recalls an instance where she herself testified before Hyde on a related matter. She spoke before the Judiciary Committee on March 11, 1997, during hearings on so-called "partial-birth abortion." Britell, a mother of two and wife of a commercial airline pilot, is Catholic and used to picket at abortion clinics. The senate hearing room chosen for the special event was packed. "I never thought I would come forward to oppose legislation on abortion," she testified. Yet Britell found out when she was six-and-a-half months pregnant in 1994 that her daughter had anacephaly, meaning she would be born without a brain and could not possibly survive outside the womb. Her doctor and the medical experts at New England Medical advised Britell to induce labor immediately, to protect her health. As a Catholic, this was unimaginable to her, and she consulted her parish priest for guidance. He said that she should listen to her doctors and he supported her and her husband's decision to end the pregnancy.

During her induced labor which should have been routine, the baby lodged in the birth canal and doctors were forced to cut the umbilical cord while the baby was still there, causing death. Under the bill Hyde and others were trying to pass, this procedure would have been illegal. "If legislation like the ban you are considering becomes law, doctors like mine at new England Medical Center could be sent to jail for acting in an emergency situation to protect a woman from injury," Britell testified.

The heartbroken mother named the baby girl Dahlia. The family buried her at a Catholic funeral performed by the parish priest. With a grief that is universal when this kind of tragedy strikes, Britell continues to mourn the loss of her daughter.

When she finished speaking, most of the hearing room was in tears. A witness who testified after Britell actually broke down herself during her testimony, and the atmosphere was highly charged with emotion. But none of it seemed to penetrate Henry Hyde, who had the air of someone unaffected.

But in the end, Hyde could not hold himself back. Adding ignorance to injury, he said to Britell, "Mrs. Britell, there is an operation that can fix that," referring to her daughter's condition. Incredulous, Brittell asked Hyde, "Are you talking about a brain transplant?" Hyde responded, "Yes." Someone came over to Hyde and whispered in his ear, likely trying to prevent further embarrassment from Hyde's "no-brainer." The conversation was glazed over.

Britell experienced first hand the irrational and dishonest lengths Hyde will take in order to protect his extremist views. And still, Hyde couldn't hold back his contempt. While discussing the issue with his colleagues over the next few minutes, he insulted Britell, calling her an "exterminator." His comment was beamed across the U.S. on C-Span, for all to hear.

Chapter 2

Sex, Lies and Truth Squads

"Well, what is an oath? An oath is an asking almighty God to witness to the truth of what you're saying."
— Henry Hyde, January 16, 1999

"We are all in danger of the religious right wing and their hypocritically false pretense at moral excellence." She hated seeing Hyde *"being so moral when he is not."* When she discovered that Hyde wrote a book on family values, *"I was struck dumb. He doesn't know the first thing about them."*
— Cherie Hancock, Henry Hyde's ex-lover

Back in October of 1968, Henry Hyde publicly made known his principled commitment to telling the truth. He and two other Republican state representatives formed what they called a "Truth Squad." It's target was a Democratic governor who had dodged inheritance taxes four years earlier. The truth squad went all out to expose the details of the skeleton in the governor's closet and charged him with "disregard and neglect of the law." Two years later, Hyde still believed he had a special handle on the truth when he attacked Adlai Stevenson, who was running for the Senate, and took it upon himself to "correct misstatements" and "finish the equations to the fractional truths" spoken by Stevenson.

50

Some people saw through Hyde's partisan antics. Tom Pugh, investigative reporter and associate editor with the *Peoria-Journal Star* at the time, remembers the truth squad very well. "There was never any doubt in anybody's mind that the truth squad was pure hypocrisy," he said in a recent interview. "It was nothing but a public relations stunt. They went around telling lies. Everybody knew that. I have no doubt that at least some of the time they lied." Even if Hyde could not fool the wiser segments of the population into thinking he was telling the truth, he seemed to have done a better job with the women in his life.

Chances are, the same day he formed the truth squad to blast his wayward opponents, Hyde spent the evening at Fritzels, the hottest dinner spot in Chicago, with his true love, Cherie Hancock. The slender, young businesswoman had been involved with the man she called "Hank" for seven years. On a typical night out on the town, the two would then hit a lively piano bar for singalongs with pianist Hots Michaels and socializing into the wee hours. When Hank arrived home and transformed into Henry Hyde, he must have concocted a pretty good lie for his wife. But lucky for him, she had probably fallen asleep many hours ago after spending the evening caring for the couple's four children.

For the eight years of this relationship, Henry Hyde did a very good job of lying to his wife and keeping her out of the picture—so good that for most of those years, Cherie Hancock did not even know he was married. "He portrayed himself as a single man. It was never brought up," she says. And Hyde had no bones about flaunting his adultery, regardless of how that might reflect on his wife. "Our relationship wasn't any secret. It was very public," Cherie said.

Cherie Hancock says that Hyde lied in his characterization of the relationship as a "youthful indiscretion" and in saying that it ended "after Mr. Snodgrass [Cherie's ex-husband] confronted my wife." Yet since the story of her relationship with Hyde broke in the Internet magazine, *Salon*, on September 16, 1998, Cherie has chosen to stay quiet about the story and has refused to respond to the barrage of press inquiries.

However, Cherie, now sixty-three, agreed to be interviewed for this book, speaking for the first time about the nature of her relationship with Henry Hyde. She also made available close family members and others who knew her and "Hank" when they were together. Independent interviews with her ex-husband, Fred Snodgrass, and another old family friend also shed light on the relationship.

The story of Hyde's extramarital relationship would never have seen the light of day if it weren't for Norman Sommer, a seventy-three-year-old retired sales executive. Sommer lives with his wife in a high-rise condo in Aventura, Florida. It so happened that he was "tennis buddies" with another retiree named Fred Snodgrass. One day, seven years before the Lewinsky scandal broke, Sommer and Snodgrass were enjoying a game of tennis on their neighborhood court. They were playing doubles with two other men. One was from Chicago and told the others that he had a men's clothing store down in the loop and mentioned that Henry Hyde was one of his customers. "Henry Hyde?" exclaimed Snodgrass. "That SOB had a five-year affair with my wife and broke up my family." Sommer was stunned. "But you know how men are, we don't sit around and gab," he said when recounting the story. "We went back to playing tennis. That's all that was ever said. When the Monica story broke, I called Fred and he gave me permission to manage the story."

Norman Sommer has been on a mission since the day Monica Lewinsky's name hit the front pages in January, 1998. He took it upon himself to set up his own truth squad exposing Henry Hyde and has been consumed with nothing else. "I knew they would try and impeach Clinton and that Hyde would be involved, so I jumped on it," he said. He has cut out every news story he could find, monitored Hyde's every move, watched all the talk shows and trial coverage, and given hours of analysis to the fine points of Hyde's contradictions and misdeeds which emerged during the impeachment hearings. He has spent thousands of hours sending out packets of information and newspaper clippings—with his own handwritten notes in the margins—to all major media and opinion makers. He's made hundreds of phone calls. But for the first seven months of his crusade, none of the media were interested. *Salon* was number fifty-seven on his list of places to pitch the story.

"I knew that Hyde was the biggest hypocrite in Washington, and that as Judiciary Committee Chairman he would play a pivotal role in any impeachment proceedings," said Sommer. "After twenty-five years of observing Henry Hyde in Congress and knowing of the adulterous, long-term affair with my tennis buddy's wife, I believed he was not qualified to be the defacto judge and part of the jury on any impeachment inquiry of our President," he said. Sommer—"an old man without any resources," as he describes himself—has truly made his mark on history.

"If the public has a right to know, in excruciating detail, about Clinton's sexual life, then surely it has an equal right to know about the private life of the man who called the family 'the surest basis of civil order, the strongest foundation for free enterprise, the safest home of freedom'..." wrote the editors of *Salon* when explaining why they chose to run the controversial story about Hyde. "Clinton is not being investigated because he had an affair, those who argue this insist, but because he lied about it. This is, we submit, either absurdly naive or disingenuous: Lying and having an affair can't be separated. To have an affair is by definition to lie about it—an affair is a lie."

Cherie Hancock did not appreciate the disruption to her life caused by the media frenzy when the story broke, which she says was painful and humiliating for both her and her husband. A full media circus descended on her suburban home in San Antonio, Texas and set up shop outside. Warned by her loyal local newspaper not to touch a blade of grass on Cherie Hancock's front lawn or she would call the police, reporters parked around the perimeter of her lawn and up and down her street for four days, ringing her doorbell about every half hour. She did not go out of her house and refused to talk. She did consent to a brief interview with the *San Antonio Express-News* and the *Dallas Morning News* solely for the purpose of setting some facts straight, and her daughter also spoke to *Salon* on her behalf.

On September 16, 1998, Hyde issued the following statement: "The statute of limitations has long since passed on my youthful indiscretions. Suffice it to say Cherie Snodgrass and I were good friends a long, long time ago. After Mr. Snodgrass confronted my wife, the friendship ended and my marriage remained intact. The only purpose for this being dredged up now is an obvious attempt to intimidate me and it won't work. I intend to fulfill my constitutional duty and deal judiciously with the serious felony allegations presented to Congress in the Starr report."

Cherie Hancock is a woman who fiercely guards her privacy and the productive life she has made for herself. She is now a publicist, writer, and dedicated volunteer for her synagogue, Hadassah and the Conference of Community and Justice, having converted from Catholicism to Judaism in 1995. She is frightened that her and her husband's lives will be scarred by another media onslaught. Yet she felt compelled to tell us her story because she feels "we are all in danger of the religious right wing and their hypocritically false pretense at moral excellence." She hated seeing Hyde "being so moral when he is not." When she discovered that Hyde wrote a book on family values, "I was struck dumb," she says. "He doesn't know the first thing about them."

The Seeds of Hypocrisy

Cherie Hancock describes an eight-year, intensely romantic and serious relationship with Henry Hyde in which the two were very much in love. "I adored him," she says. "We showered each other with love." Hancock was legally separated from her husband when she started going with Hyde, and her divorce was finalized by the end of the first two years. She does not solely blame Hyde, as does her ex-husband, for the breakup of what she describes as an already troubled marriage. "Hank was the catalyst," she says. "Without him I would have had a harder time emotionally, because I never really wanted to

Lying under oath? What oath? Hank and Cherie in a Chicago nightclub. Hyde had a serious, long-term relationship with businesswoman Cherie Hancock while he was married, raising four children, and going to church on Sundays.

split up my family. It took this catalyst to free myself from what was, for me, a very unhappy marriage. Hank helped me realize there was more to life. He was sunshine in my life. It was like coming out of a dungeon into a bright field full of flowers when I met him."

By her account, the relationship began in 1961, when she was twenty-five-and-a-half and Hyde was thirty-seven. Although her ex-husband reported to *Salon* that the relationship began in 1965 and lasted five years, he acknowledged in a February interview that "it very easily could have gone on longer, I don't know." A close relative of Cherie Hancock's, who wished to remain anonymous for this book, confirmed the beginning of the relationship as 1961. Cherie had three small children and had just become financially independent, eventually owning multiple beauty salons. Hyde was a lawyer at the time, operating out of a small office on LaSalle Street while launching his career in politics. He was elected to the state legislature in 1966.

When she first started dating Hyde, Cherie says that many people tried to persuade her to drop him. Hyde already had a reputation as a womanizer. The attorney who shared an office with Hyde, Norman Gross, was also her good friend. He warned her about getting close to Hyde. "Stay away from him, he's trouble," he said in his office one day. Prior to their relationship, Cherie says that Hyde was having an affair with his secretary, Miriam, and that she and many others saw them together. "I remember Miriam at one time showing the mink stole he had bought her to some acquaintances," says Cherie. Hank and Cherie were in the same social circle and knew each other before becoming involved. They frequented the same nightspots, where Cherie said she used to see him with Miriam. "Hank seemed very attracted to me and I to him," she says. "One day we got together for dinner and I asked him about Miriam. He said he wasn't seeing her anymore. And that was the start of a beautiful romance for the two of us."

Cherie ignored the counsel of the more experienced people around Hyde. "I didn't realize I was too young and naive to be able to handle myself with him. I chose not to believe these stories." Instead, she leapt into the romance. "There was a wonderful side to Henry Hyde," she says. "He was charming, thoughtful, giving and brilliant and had the most wonderful sense of humor." As the relationship developed, Hyde even became friendly with Cherie's family. He went on a Yacht party given by Cherie's ex-brother-in-law. Hyde knew her mother, father, siblings and three children. "Henry met her parents at their home," confirmed Hancock's relative. "He didn't do holidays with us because he spent them with his children. But he spent Christmas Eve with Cherie every year they were together." Hyde also went on vacations with members of Hancock's family. On one occasion he spent four or five days in New Orleans for a planned vacation with some of her family, she said.

Hyde was not concerned about hiding his adulterous relationship and was seen in public with Cherie for years. "His wife never was anywhere," says Cherie. "We went to political fund-raisers and rallies together. I knew his friends, which included attorneys, legislators and people from all walks of life, and sometimes we went out to dinner with them and went to all the night spots that Chicago was famous for. That's why I never thought he was married." Cherie did know that he had kids, but assumed he was divorced. "He never saw them; he was out all the time" she says. "He was free as a butterfly. He seemed freer than a single man."

She says fantasies of marriage came up in their conversations. But she was not happy with Hyde's image of a wife. "He had double standards for men and women," she said. "He liked to picture a woman at home with a gardening hat on, doing feminine things." She didn't think she could be satisfied with marriage. "Inside, I thought marriage would mean staying at home with seven children while Hank was away in the Capitol, and me being left behind." Even so, "He had a fantasy of us being married and going to church with me every Sunday," she said.

Despite the fact that he was committing the sin of adultery, Hyde's Catholicism was in the picture a great deal. "Sometimes I would get fed up with all his hypocrisies. I don't think he's any more Catholic than anybody else. How could he go to church every Sunday, or confession? It was just a joke, for show. I think it was to show his kids." Cherie recalls him making light of his faith. "He called me 'my heathen' because I told him I didn't believe in all that hocus pocus," she says. She remembers a prayer that he used to say at parties, as a joke—"Dear God, make me pure, but not now, later." And everybody would laugh, including her.

Hyde's prayer must have been answered, since he grew so pure that even birth control became "morally wrong" by his standards. He was granted a private audience with the Pope at the Vatican in 1994, and a year later became a "papal knight."

Cherie remembers well how shocked she was when Hyde passed the Hyde Amendment, denying Medicaid to poor women for abortions, shortly after landing himself in Congress. "I was extremely shocked and disgusted, because of the hypocrisy," she says. "That Hyde amendment tells human beings that they can't do what they want with their own bodies. That is dictatorship. Henry Hyde wants to hurt people by taking away their rights, exactly like the religious right wing," she says.

But before he started passing legislation harmful to women, Cherie remembers wonderful times with Hank—nights out at Chicago's finest night clubs and piano bars, yacht parties, trips to the state capital staying in lovely hotels, ten days on the east coast where she remembers teaching him to waltz. "We never had to be with anybody or specifically anywhere to be happy together," she says. But she also believes the seeds of what Hyde was to become were already there. "He used to try and hide his intolerance towards people of a different ilk, because I was not that way. I suspected all those extremely negative things about him, but I shoved them aside and said 'no, it can't be.'" When he made it into politics, she was not surprised to see how he turned out. "When the Clinton thing came about, I could see the magnification of the little tiny glimpses I got when I was going with him that I would put out of my mind because they were distasteful to me. I had seen too many glimpses of his intolerance. You name it, he was intolerant. I think he was just as bad back then really; he just didn't have the marketplace to show it."

A Family Affair

Fred Snodgrass lays the blame on Hyde for destroying his marriage and damaging his relationship with his three children. Today, Snodgrass lives alone in a tiny, subsidized apartment in Weston, Florida. A seventy-six-year-old retired furniture salesman, he works a couple of times a week at the local recreational department swimming pool, a necessity if he is to make ends meet. When he turned on his television during the height of the impeachment hearings, he couldn't quite believe what he saw. "That big guy that I watch on TV is the same man who had an affair with my wife," he says.

Fred Snodgrass has many painful memories of the years when his life was haunted by Henry Hyde and when he was consumed by trying to rid his family of

Hyde's presence. He breaks down in tears when he talks about his children, who he felt he lost when Cherie took them to California after she broke up with Hyde. Two of them still won't talk to him. He says he has nothing against his ex-wife now, but agreed to reveal the story through his friend Norman Sommer because of Henry Hyde's double standard, and because Hyde had not been held accountable. "He thinks he's beyond the law and he can do what he wants to do," says Snodgrass.

He remembers a few uncomfortable incidents when he saw his ex-wife with Hyde. Cherie was a hair model and used to travel to beauty shows in different cities. One time Fred drove her to the airport and insisted on carrying her bags to the gate. "As we were getting close to the gate," Fred says, "she said something like, 'I don't like the way you're dressed, you don't look good' trying to make me turn back, and that's when I saw him. Henry Hyde. He was standing there waiting for her, looking out from the gate." Cherie says she also remembers that time when the three paths crossed.

Alex Berke is an old family friend who knew Snodgrass even before he and Cherie were married, which happened when Cherie was only eighteen. "They were a beautiful couple. She was gorgeous, that Cherie, a lot of personality, and Freddie was a hell of a good looking guy," he says. He too holds Hyde responsible for destroying the marriage and breaking up "a good home."

Berke, a thirty-eight year veteran of the Chicago Board of Trade, was outraged by the spectacle of Henry Hyde sitting in lofty judgment of President Clinton. "Hyde speaks about trust. When he got married, did he give his wife his trust? Did he take an oath that he would never cheat on her and be honest with her? Is there any difference between an oath of marriage and putting your hand on a Bible? I can't see any difference," he says.

Sometimes he had to turn off the TV in disgust. "His lying and his violation of trust makes him the biggest hypocrite in the world. What the hell did he tell his wife all those nights he was out with Cherie? That he was out picking up firewood for somebody? Out picking oranges? When his wife died, she probably died of a broken heart."

Fred Snodgrass decided after a number of years that Hyde's wife Jeanne should know about the secret affair. He called Hyde's office and got his home address from the secretary, saying he wanted to send a personal invitation to a social event. When she opened the door, Fred was surprised that Jeanne Hyde invited him in. "Hyde's wife was a kind of motherly, homebody type with graying hair," said Fred. "The complete opposite of Cherie." According to Fred, he told her that Cherie was off in Springfield with her husband. Defensive at first, she said "He's a brilliant man and she's a tramp." Then she began to cry. She called the hotel in Springfield where Hyde had told her he would be staying. He wasn't even registered. "She was sobbing," he says. Snodgrass suggested they get into his car and drive to Springfield, but she declined, saying she had a young child to care for.

Cherie was with Hyde in Springfield when Fred paid this fateful visit to the Hyde home—one of many trips the couple took to the state capital when Hyde was a representative. They always stayed at "very lovely" hotels. Sometimes Cherie went to the legislature and sat and listened, "but that was pretty boring and repetitious. They never got anything done anyway," she says. More often, while he was at the State House, Cherie would amuse herself by shopping, swimming, relaxing at the hotel, or going to a show. She remembers the day when she first found out that the love of her life had a wife, thanks to the interference of her jealous ex-husband. Hancock was enjoying the hotel room after lunch time. She was surprised when Hyde suddenly walked into the room, back from the legislature earlier than usual. He said, "Fred went to see my wife last night." As Hancock remembers it, she said nothing. "I was shocked, speechless."

They got in the car and drove back to Chicago. "I felt physically sick and my mind was spinning," says Cherie. "I know he did a lot of talking, but God knows, I don't remember what he said. It was probably the worst day of my life. I was too shocked to say anything," she says. He took her home and returned to his family. During six years of an extremely close relationship, Hyde had never told Cherie he was married. "Nobody had any idea what I was going through, including him," she remembers. According to Cherie, this did not put a damper on the relationship for very long. "We just drifted back to where we were within a week. The issue of him being married was never discussed," she recalls. "Morally, it wasn't right of me to date him after I knew he was married. But those remaining years were marvelous."

Lying About Sex

It is clear to Cherie Hancock and her family members that knew the couple well that Henry Hyde, now having more fully developed his "dark, murky side," lied in his public statement about the type of relationship this was when *Salon* exposed it in 1998. First of all, the characterization "youthful indiscretion" is obviously not applicable to a long-term, serious and romantic relationship in which Hyde took vacations with members of his partner's family. And he was not particularly youthful, being forty-five years old and an accomplished state representative by the time the relationship ended. That's just five years younger than Clinton was at the time of his liaison with Lewinsky.

Cherie Hancock was disgusted with the cowardice of his explanation. "It's a lie. Of course it's a lie," she says. "The word 'indiscretion' is an insult. There is absolutely no question that he was lying to the public in that statement." Her family member also says Hyde lied about the nature of the relationship. "Seven or eight years? Some youthful indiscretion."

Hyde also lied, according to Hancock and the family member, when he stated that "after Mr. Snodgrass confronted my wife, the friendship ended." This is a denial of the more disturbing fact that he continued his public, adulterous relationship for years, even after his wife found out. He said, "My marriage remained intact." Cherie's explanation is that this statement "is for show. He is a showman as everybody who knows him knows. This was for the benefit only of his colleagues and the media," she says.

Cherie remembers without a doubt that she and Hank were together at least two years after Jeanne Hyde found out, and that they broke up in 1969. She was thirty-three and Hank was forty-five at the time. The cause of the breakup was not that Mrs. Hyde found out, but was due to something "very serious" that happened between them. When the story broke, Fred Snodgrass told *Salon* that his visit with Jeanne Hyde was in the fall of 1969 and that Hyde broke up with Cherie the next day. Hyde may have found it convenient to go along with that scenario. But Cherie and a close family member place these two pivotal events which they will never forget—Cherie's discovery that Hank was married and the breakup—years apart. And Cherie corrected her ex-husband's statement to *Salon*, speaking through her daughter, the day after they ran the Snodgrass version of the story with Hyde's statement included.

Cherie's close relative remembers talking to Cherie both when she learned that Hyde was married and also when she called, devastated, at the time they broke up. "I remember when Henry's wife found out. Cherie's reaction was that she was very angry at Fred for doing that. She said, 'Why would Fred do that? It doesn't hurt Hank. It doesn't hurt me. It hurts her.' She was not worried about breaking up then. That's the reaction I remember." The family member also remembers that significant time had passed when she got Cherie's call that they were breaking up. "The wife finding out was not what broke them up. That was old news by then," said this close relative. "I remember Cherie's call about it and that was not it." Cherie has vowed to keep the cause of the breakup private.

Cherie was disturbed watching the impeachment hearings and seeing what her former love has become. "I don't hate him. I hate what he wants to do to the people of the United States. I hate the dark murky side of him where he wants people to live as he sees fit. He's being so moralistic when he was just the opposite. And 'youthful indiscretion' was the topper, because our romance was so intensely serious for both of us. And when I saw the arrogance on his face at the impeachment hearings it made me sick."

Meanwhile, Fred Snodgrass and at least one of his daughters have acknowledged that they still carry wounds from the impact of Hyde's relationship with Cherie on the life of their family. Hyde never chose to affirm family values by publicly saying that he has any regrets, either to the members of his own family or to hers.

Calling in the FBI: "Pure and Simple Intimidation"

The day before the news of his adultery broke, Henry Hyde was obviously already worried. He wrote a letter to his fellow Judiciary Committee members warning them that Clinton supporters may be gathering personal information about members of the committee for the purpose of embarrassing them. He threatened to refer the suspicious characters to the Justice Department, saying that efforts to "intimidate" members of Congress would constitute a federal crime and could land the offender five years in jail. "The only purpose for this being dredged up now is an obvious attempt to intimidate me, and it won't work." He told his fellow members, "I request that you immediately notify me if you learn of any activity or information relating to this concern." Since the letter was released to the press, his accusations of criminal action were clearly designed to intimidate, even though at the same time he was complaining that he himself was the victim of intimidation.

Although Hyde and a number of his Republican colleagues seemed convinced that the White House was out to get them by releasing the story of Hyde's affair—and publicly said so—it quickly became clear that the information that went from Norman Sommer to *Salon* had absolutely nothing to do with the White House. Yet this did not stop a group of Republicans from sending a letter to FBI director Louis J. Freeh complaining about "smear tactics" and "pure and simple intimidation." They requested an investigation into the "certain individuals" who had been dredging up information embarrassing to members of Congress.

White House spokesperson Mike McCurry responded that any staffers who had participated in the disclosure about Hyde would be fired. "We gave Chairman Hyde personal assurances that these things would not happen," McCurry said.

The individual targeted above all others, and for weeks, was White House assistant Sidney Blumenthal. Republican leaders claimed that Blumenthal had arranged for the Hyde story to surface, and they demanded an FBI investigation into his activities. Even though they admitted they had no proof of Blumenthal's participation, the Republicans fueled a round of press attacks on him which seemed to leave no doubt as to his guilt. This was despite Norman Sommer being the source of the story, and his clear statement that he had never talked to Blumenthal or to anyone else at the White House.

Norman Sommer remembers being unnerved by Hyde's threat of FBI probes and jail sentences. He first heard about Hyde's statement while watching CNN's *Burden of Proof* on September 16. Greta van Sustern, the host, was suddenly handed a press release from Hyde's office stating the same threats that were made in his letter to the Judiciary Committee. She read parts of it over the air. "This announcement sent a chill up and down my spine," he says. "I picked up the phone and called the national headquarters of the ACLU." He labels this extreme action "McCarthyism revisited." "This was a blatant abuse of congressional power intended to intimidate and suppress private citizens' first amendment rights of free speech. It is particularly ironic given the tactics taken by Starr and relished by Hyde to expose Clinton's indiscretions in gory detail," he said.

Right after the story broke, Norman Sommer was interviewed extensively on television and radio. But soon thereafter the hate mail began arriving, and when he heard that *Salon* had received a bomb threat, that was the last straw. He suggested to his wife that she move in with her daughter or that he move out, until "this terror threat" diminished. Instead of taking such drastic action, he stopped granting interviews and cut back his political activities—but only temporarily.

Love the Sinner—
But Only if He's a Conservative Republican

When moralizing about the sexual affairs of other elected officials, Hyde has picked his self-serving positions carefully.

In 1982, he participated in a scenario with amazing parallels to the Starr/Clinton affair. Former Jimmy Carter Cabinet member Joseph Califano assumed the role of special counsel in a House Ethics Committee probe looking into possible sex scandals involving members of Congress. One year and $1.5 million later, Califano released a damning report charging, among other things, conservative Illinois Representative Dan Crane with having had an illicit sexual affair with a 17-year-old girl—which constitutes statutory rape in most states—who was working as an unpaid congressional page. Details of the sexual affair were spelled out in a report written by Special Counsel Califano, described by *Roll Call*, the newspaper of Capitol Hill, as "softcore compared with the report by independent counsel Kenneth Starr." Nonetheless, it included interviews with hundreds of teenage pages, and was shocking enough in its day. Califano vowed that "improper behavior" by public officials "should not be understated or excused. It must be rooted out vigorously, promptly and publicly."

Crane had no choice but to admit to the affair. He begged his wife, six kids, staff, constituency, and party for forgiveness, but vowed amidst calls for his resignation that he would not step down. The matter came to the floor of a full House on July 20, 1983. Days earlier, the bipartisan Ethics Committee had voted to reprimand Crane, but leading the charge for Crane's expulsion was fellow Republican Newt Gingrich. Things were looking grim for Crane, but the tide of expulsion was turned thanks to a floor speech by Henry Hyde in Crane's defense. Hyde pleaded with the House to censure instead of expel Crane.

"We sit here not to characterize the crime, the breach, the transgression, because we all know the transgression, which is admitted and it is stipulated as reprehensible," expounded Hyde. Hyde could have been consoling himself, but it is likely he never imagined his own transgression would be revealed. "He is embarrassed, he is humiliated, he is displaced," he said of Crane. "It will be with him, and it will be with his family as long as they live…" His ultimate plea for Crane was couched in piousness. "…Mr. Speaker, I suggest to the members that compassion and justice are not antithetical; they are complimentary. The Judeo-Christian tradition says, 'Hate the sin and love the sinner.' We are on record as hating the sin, some more ostentatiously than others. I think it is time to love the sinner."

Hyde's eloquence served him well, and his friend Crane was not removed from office due to Hyde's ability to sway the Congress. Hyde played a pivotal role, as he did in Clinton's impeachment, but this time he was on the opposite side of the fence. The House voted only to censure Dan Crane, but he still lost his upcoming election.

Crane was never formally accused of lying about his affair, which is of course the sin that Hyde claimed was Clinton's. Many believe that this argument is thin and was simply a cover for a partisan attack, with the dubious claim of lying under oath as a shield. "The case before you, Senators, is not about sexual misconduct, infidelity, adultery," said Hyde in his January 1999 summation to the Senate. "Those are private acts and are none of our business. It's not even a question of lying about sex. The matter before this body is a question of lying under oath," he said.

But it seems there was at least some lying going on in Crane's case. "They didn't come forward. They were not volunteers," said Richard Cotton, who served as a deputy counsel under Califano in the investigation. He was referring to Crane and another victim of the inquisition, democrat Gerry Studs. "It took a good deal of investigative work in that all of the individuals involved in terms of their colleagues had generally, obviously created cover stories and conducted themselves where this was being concealed as opposed to advertised." According to Califano's report, Crane did not admit to the affair until his second deposition. At the beginning of the investigation, a year before the information was disclosed, Crane made sure to let it be known he wasn't one of the accused. "I hope investigators use discretion and if they can prove it, I hope they sock it to them and throw them out," he said.

If Crane had been accused of lying under oath, would this mean that it was no longer time to love the sinner, according to Hyde? Just a few years later, Hyde condoned his friend Oliver North's lies under oath about issues much more important than sex. And he certainly didn't seem to hate his own sin back in his carefree days with Cherie Hancock.

Chapter 3

A Bandit on the
Bank Board

Henry Hyde is a man of many scandals. So many that on some days they seem to collide. On November 19, 1998 as House Judiciary Chairman, he played the role of prosecutor, swearing in Independent Counsel Kenneth Starr to make the case for impeaching President Clinton. Also on that very day came an editorial from his home newspaper, *The Chicago Tribune*. It called for a thorough investigation into a different scandal: Hyde's dealings as a board member of Clyde Federal Savings and Loan Association, in North Riverside, Illinois, and for a House Ethics Committee probe into why he hired a private investigator to keep tabs on a local whistle-blower. There is "the need for Hyde to account fully for his Clyde Federal activities and his private eye," the editorial stated. "An investigation as momentous as a Presidential Impeachment is ill-served by clouds hovering over the head of the committee doing the investigating. And the silence of the Ethics Committee in this matter is deafening."

If Clinton's cover-up of his relationship with Monica Lewinsky was the scandal of the 90s, the S&L crisis was the scandal of the 80s. Henry Hyde will go down in history as a central figure prosecuting Clinton. But through the 80s he helped propel a fiscal debacle that would cost taxpayers $200 billion—a figure that is still rising a decade later.

S&L deposits are insured against bankruptcy by the Federal Deposit Insurance Corporation (FDIC). Prior to 1982, S&L investments were tightly regulated to safeguard depositors', and ultimately the taxpayers' money.

But all this changed in 1982, with the passage of Garn St. Germain deregulation legislation, which while keeping deposit insurance intact, scrapped crucial regulations on how that money could be invested. Where once S&Ls were locally controlled institutions with deep roots in the community, suddenly they were free to invest depositors' cash elsewhere, secure in the knowledge that if the investments failed, the FDIC would pick up the tab. S&L's became personalized cash cows for a legion of high-rolling entrepreneurs, swindlers and backroom dealers.

Consider post de-reg high-roller, Ed McBirney. "Fast Eddie" offered a clear contrast to the typical nine-to-five S&L banker providing low interest mortgage loans to his neighbors. While McBirney was not big on community investments, he certainly knew how to throw a bash for his clients. His lavish affairs included expensive parties and feasts where roast lion was served. McBirney, who gambled excessively and invested in Rolls Royces, once turned an old warehouse into a mock African jungle with a live elephant. McBirney was able to hire a magician to make the elephant disappear, but he would need much more than a little stage magic to make his legal problems go away. Ultimately, McBirney's Sunbelt Savings had to be bailed out for the astonishing sum of $2 billion.

Jesse James would have been jealous. By the time the dust had started to settle at the end of the 1980s, this new breed of banking bandit had blown billions in federally insured money, investing in everything from junk-bonds and race horses to windmills in the desert. Some banks even fronted for spies, drug lords and arms smugglers.

On a crisp fall day in 1982, surrounded by bankers, lobbyists and their political pawns in Congress, President Reagan signed S&L deregulation into law and threw open the doors of America's S&Ls to a new breed of bank robber eager to invest depositors' money at the tax-payers' risk. These modern day bandits needed no guns, dynamite, or blue-prints passed along by cooperating insiders. They were the insiders and Henry Hyde was one of them.

Henry and Clyde

Hyde outdid many of his colleagues in Congress who just cheered on deregulation when the price was right. While the Illinois congressman did receive over $115,000 in campaign contributions and speaking fees from the banking community, this was not nearly enough for Hyde. He went well beyond giving speeches, backing industry-friendly legislation and accepting campaign donations, and opted for the keys to the vault. Hyde took the unusual step in 1981 of joining Clyde's Board of Directors, while still serving in Congress. The request that he become a board member came from Clyde's chairman, Sylvia Miedema, who according to Federal election records, contributed $5,850 to Hyde's campaigns between 1981 and 1989. Hyde apparently returned the favor by voting to raise Miedema's salary after he joined the board. But it certainly wasn't only Miedema who gained from Hyde's pro-industry ties. Between 1980 and 1992, Hyde voted to support seven major pieces of legis-lation to deregulate S&Ls and greatly enrich the bank accounts of S&L officers and directors all across the country.

Prior to Hyde's arrival, Clyde was like most federally insured "thrifts," a modest community bank founded to provide low-cost mortgage loans that would enable a young couple to purchase its first house. But Clyde's direction would change dramatically during Hyde's tenure. The S&L was dragged from making predictable and safe home mortgages into risky out-of-state investments. By the time Hyde had washed his hands of Clyde in 1984, the S&L was well on the way to insolvency, eventually leaving taxpayers to pick up the tab for a $67 million bailout. Hyde's wheeling and dealing on Clyde's board would earn him the unique honor of being the only sitting congressman to be sued by federal regulators burdened with the enormous task of cleaning up ten years of deregulated banking.

Hyde says he gained very little as a board member of Clyde other than a $300 per month stipend, but minutes of several board meetings indicate a fertile potential for personal benefits by board members. At a September 27, 1982 meeting, Hyde seconded a motion that offered special loans to board members and others. The motion, approved by the board, made "mortgage loans to its directors, advisory directors, officers and employees at an interest rate of 2% over the association's cost of funds or 1/2% below current market rate at the time of application, whichever is lower," according to the minutes. This was particularly shocking, because Hyde was in essence voting to violate a law that he supported and was passed by Congress in 1978, when he was a member of the banking committee. The Hyde-supported legislation barred financial institutions from offering directors or officers more favorable credit terms than were being offered to the general public.

In the aftermath of the bankruptcy and bailout, a key question remains: just how central was Hyde in the slide of Clyde? Central enough that on April 27, 1993, the Resolution Trust Corporation of America (RTC), a federal agency created by Congress to manage and litigate the S&L bailout, filed a $17.2 million federal civil lawsuit against Hyde and eleven others at Clyde Federal. Even under the relatively lax regulatory atmosphere of Garn St. Germain deregulation legislation, Hyde and his crew from Clyde were cited for "negligence, gross negligence, mismanagement, breach of fiduciary and other duties, breach of contract and other wrongful and improper conduct." The Clyde defendants, according to the RTC suit, "carelessly...mismanaged Clyde, caused or permitted Clyde to violate federal regulations, and ignored warnings, recommendations and/or directives of Federal Regulatory Agencies."

The 1993 lawsuit went further, directly implicating Hyde in a wide array of risky options deals, that "the defendants knew or should have known...would have dire consequences to Clyde...The defendants breached their respective duties by negligently, carelessly, recklessly, imprudently, with gross negligence...failing to exercise due care, skill and diligence in the management, monitoring, administration, and supervision of Clyde."

Hyde's account of his roll is starkly different. He paints his participation as only slightly more than tangential. Far from being in the know about putting Clyde and its depositors at risk, Hyde implies that though he was a former member of the House Banking Committee, his motions and seconding motions which jeopardized tens of millions of dollars were based on nothing more than his desire "to move the meeting along." Outside the Clyde loop, he was a virtual figurehead tied to the whims of others.

Tell it to the judge. U.S. District Court Judge Brian Barnett Duff, a former Republican colleague of Hyde's in the Illinois Legislature, saw Hyde's role differently. In a December 1995 decision, Duff sustained the RTC's most serious claim of gross negligence against Hyde, and refused to cut him loose from the suit, despite the considerable fight waged by Hyde's legal team. Judge Duff's refusal to dismiss the gross negligence charge was backed up by a three judge panel of the 7th U.S. Circuit Court of Appeals and with good reason.

Federal court documents and minutes to Clyde's board meetings, obtained through Freedom of Information Act requests, make clear why the judge didn't buy it. They reveal a troubling picture of the Chairman's direct involvement in illegal deals that wasted millions. The federal regulators in their lawsuit against Hyde put it this way: "At all relevant times prior to February 1, 1990, the defendant directors comprised a majority of Clyde's Board and the defendants controlled and dominated the actions and decisions of Clyde." Leaving no wiggle room for claims of being out of the loop, the suit further stated, "During the time when defendants controlled Clyde, they were vested with control over the causes of action asserted herein."

It was only after Duff, Hyde's self-proclaimed friend, alerted the defendants that they were trial bound, that the case was actually settled.

Having put forth an utterly unconvincing argument that he was out of the loop, Hyde also has repeatedly claimed that the bank was not in trouble during the years he was responsible for it. This claim also stands the truth on its head. Red flags started popping up at Clyde as early as 1982, when Hyde and the other board members were informed by the Federal Home Loan Bank Board that their S&L had about thirteen or fourteen months to insolvency. Hyde was well aware that the bank was in serious trouble, yet he kept pushing the S&L into increasingly risky transactions.

According to a highly critical November 28, 1983 letter from outside auditors at Cobitz, Vandenburg and Fennessy, Clyde was in a shambles and heading for bankruptcy. Tim Anderson, a fifty-six-year-old independent banking consultant, put the matter this way: "The outside auditor's report was so devastating," says Anderson, "that when the board read the report they should have told management to leave the room and the remaining outside directors should have had a meeting to decide either to replace management immediately or to resign in protest, but they went ahead and did nothing. Now Henry is going to claim he knew nothing about this, but the regulatory people said in writing that Henry signed the letter stating that he had read the report. Henry knew how bad this thrift was while he was on board, he knew it was insolvent and he knew it was failing." Anderson is former Marine and Republican committeeman who has been investigating Hyde's conduct for over a decade.

In a Clyde board meeting on October, 17, 1983, Hyde seconded a motion that transferred $287,625 from Clyde to Clyde's employees' profit sharing plan and trust. But unfortunately for Clyde, there were no profits to share. According to the Congressional Accountability

Project (CAP), a Washington watchdog group, "Clyde was not making any profits. In fact, it was losing money quickly. Chairman Hyde and other members of the board were irresponsible in transferring this money to the employees' profit sharing plan."

According to Anderson, Clyde's board depended on Hyde's guidance and political savvy. "Board members looked to Hyde for leadership because of his knowledge not just as a lawyer and the future head of Judiciary...but as a former member of House Banking with considerable expertise." Anderson claimed that Hyde pushed the S&L into disastrous decisions. "It was Hyde who got them to invest millions of dollars in a Dallas office project that could not go forward...Hyde was the ringleader."

Investing for Dummies: The Hyde Guide

Bank records directly implicate Hyde in approving a highly speculative out-of-state options trading scheme. Minutes of a September 26, 1983 meeting of Clyde's board reveal that the man who became Judiciary Chairman actually seconded the motion that blindly plunged Clyde into a series of treacherous and costly options transactions. "RESOLVED, That the appropriate officers listed below are hereby authorized and directed...to engage in the use of options transactions...the following persons are hereby individually authorized to execute options transactions on behalf of the Association." Listed among those given authority by Hyde and the other board members to risk millions in federally insured dollars was Hyde friend and consistent campaign contributor, Sylvia A. Miedema, Chairman of the Board and Clyde Chief Executive Officer.

The options deal turned into an expensive disaster, and was a key reason why Hyde was cited by the Feds for gross negligence. According to Federal regulators, "The Clyde board failed to promulgate appropriate options writing policies" despite repeated warnings from regulators about Clyde's "improper record-keeping, absence of limits on options trading and violations of applicable Federal Law." Worse, according to the RTC complaint, "No one on Clyde's Board or employed by Clyde had any prior experience in this speculative activity in 1983."

Most significantly, regulators began warning Clyde officials as early as December of 1983, only two months after the Clyde board jumped into the abyss of options trading. But the prescient warning was ignored. According to federal court documents, "As a result of the Board's...failure to properly supervise this activity, heed Federal Home Loan Bank Board criticisms, and follow the applicable federal regulations, Clyde experienced losses in excess of $10 million from options trading."

But the FDIC suit may not have gone far enough. Among the surprising revelations in the 1983 Cobitz, Vandenburg and Fennessy audit, was the fact that Hyde and his Clyde colleagues appeared to be bilking the Federal Treasury out of interest on student loans. The audit states that "it appears that [Clyde] is overcharging the government for interest on student loans." "Chairman Hyde should have been acutely sensitive to this issue because he is a member of Congress and a former member of the House Banking Committee," says Gary Ruskin of CAP. "Did the FDIC ever investigate Clyde's apparent bilking of the taxpayers by overcharging the federal government for interest on student loans? If not, why not?"

A Bandit on the Bank Board

Hyde and Swink: Another Special Investment

At a May 17, 1982 Clyde board meeting, Hyde seconded a motion to purchase risky securities through Swink & Co., run by Jimmy Dale Swink, Sr. of Little Rock, Arkansas. While Swink's resume should have caused Clyde's board immediate concern, Hyde was seconding a motion to jump into a multimillion-dollar off-shore certificate of deposit banking deal with a man in the process of becoming one of America's preeminent white-collar criminals.

Swink & Co. had a reputation as a second-rate securities house, a "bucket shop," says Tim Anderson. "Swink should have been avoided like the plague...You're not supposed to be in the business of playing with your community customers' government insured deposits with the likes of Jimmy Swink..."

Swink certainly had an impressive record when it came to misleading his clients and wasting millions of other people's money. According to numerous published reports and an investigation by the Congressional Accountability Project, Swink had a white-collar rap sheet of Securities Law violations.

On November 30, 1984, Swink was fined $50,000 by the National Association of Securities Dealers (NASD) for failing to maintain adequate net capital, making false statements in an advertisement, and other violations. On February 21, 1984, the U.S. District Court in Little Rock permanently forbade Swink from further violations of Securities and Exchange Commission (SEC) rules regarding net capital requirements, record-keeping and other rules.

In July of 1989, the *Bond Buyer* reported that the National Association of Securities Dealers had levied a

$50,000 fine on Swink & Co. According to the paper, "The association accused Mr. Swink and his firm of inaccurate net capital computation and reporting and of engaging in the securities business while failing the minimum required net capital." And according to *Bond Buyer*, "The NASD considers violation of the minimum net capital rule to be extremely serious.".

In 1989, *Forbes* magazine revealed that "Swink & Co. has had no fewer than twenty-four municipal bond defaults since 1983, worth in excess of $120 million." Swink was eventually barred from the securities business in 1993 after he pleaded guilty to conspiracy to commit securities fraud. He ended up serving twenty-one months in an Arkansas correctional facility." Hyde continued to support the investments with Swink all the way through until his departure from the Clyde board in 1984.

"Any thorough investigation of Clyde," says Gary Ruskin, director of CAP, "would have to include a careful analysis of how the various transactions were arranged between Swink and Clyde and who was doing the arranging." Ruskin is particularly curious about Clyde's leap into the secretive world of offshore banking. "Did the FDIC ever investigate the strange circumstances of this Illinois S&L's involvement with Grand Cayman CDs, which could conceivably involve money laundering activities? If not, why not?"

The securities deal between Clyde and Swink & Co. included $2,875,000 in eurodollars funneled through a Grand Cayman Islands bank. "I don't know why Hyde would want to do this unless he was trying to funnel money to the Contras or something," says an irate Tim Anderson. "The man is well educated in high finance. As a former member of the House Banking Committee,

Henry must have understood the connotation of buying Grand Cayman CDs. The Cayman Islands has a reputation as a place to launder money; it is offshore money. The idea of the Grand Cayman CDs is this: someone who has money he doesn't want acknowledged, either drug money, gambling money, or money siphoned off, for example; they take the money, fly it to the Cayman Islands, deposit, say, $100,000 in currency. It is now sitting in a Grand Cayman branch. He wants the money back here, so he brings it back in the form of a CD. When the CD comes into the country, it's not cash, it's just a CD…This is a big red flag.

"A good lawyer," said Anderson, "would get up and take a walk if they were going to do something like buy Cayman Island CDs from a crook like Swink. If I were a U.S. Congressman, who had just been on the House Banking Committee and knew all about Grand Cayman CDs, I would have insisted that we stop doing that instantly or I'm off this board."

But not Chairman Hyde. In fact, Hyde appears to have been mesmerized by his new power to invest with the big players in the offshore market. And the minutes of an October 1982 meeting revealed Hyde again encouraging other investments with Swink.

Loosing with Luxury

Jimmy Dale Swink was not the only shady character Clyde jumped into bed with at the direction of Henry Hyde. Among those also entrusted with Clyde's future was J. William Oldenburg. a white-collar wheeler and dealer with a checkered past. Clyde's failed joint venture in luxury Texas condos with Oldenburg would ultimately cost Clyde close to $4 million.

Oldenburg was a San Francisco entrepreneur and former owner of a professional football team. He had been charged with inflating land values to defraud a Salt Lake City S&L of more than $20 million. He was tried on two occasions, but in both instances the jury failed to reach a verdict. In 1974, Oldenburg was charged by the Securities and Exchange Commission (SEC) with fraud. *The Wall Street Journal* reported that the case was settled by consent order.

In *Inside Job: The Looting of America's Savings and Loans*, co-authors Stephen Pizzo, Mary Fricker and Paul Muolo paint an interesting portrait of Oldenburg, a central figure in the demise of Clyde. Oldenburg was alleged to have links with organized crime through his close ties with the San Carlos-based Eureka Federal Savings. Eureka financed casinos in Las Vegas. *Inside Job* attests that the Feds sued Oldenburg and others for "$50 million, alleging fraud and self-dealing." In 1989, Oldenberg was indicted by the San Francisco United States Attorney for "grossly inflating the value of land so he and others could sell it to State Savings at an enormous profit," says *Inside Job*.

Clyde's association with Oldenburg reached a key point in 1984. At a board meeting on February 27, Clyde's directors voted unanimously to approve the purchase of $5 million of the $28.5 million loan to build the Aransas Princess luxury condominium project in Port Aransas, Texas. The loan purchase was brokered by Oldenburg, through Guaranty Savings and Loan Association of Harrison, Arkansas. Guaranty, like Clyde National, was a small town S&L when Oldenburg came to its "rescue" and involved it in risky out-of-state investments.

A Bandit on the Bank Board

Guaranty went bankrupt in 1989, costing taxpayers $82 million. The Arkansas S&L's failure killed the Texas condo project. This in turn cost Clyde in excess of $3.7 million. The Feds' complaint was similar to its point about options trading. With no oversight or questioning from the board, Clyde had let Oldenburg hustle millions in federally insured funds out of its hands in one astounding move. "Clyde did little or none of its own underwriting in connection with the Aransas Princess loan," stated federal investigators. "Instead, the defendants relied upon information provided and analyzed by a broker who stood to receive a substantial fee if the Aransas Princess loan were made. The information and analysis of the broker was insufficient and improper." That broker was Oldenburg.

"Henry had a track record of doing business with con-men," says Anderson, "and they did continuous business with Oldenburg as late as 1984, when top regulators in Washington were running around Congress saying the sky is falling in Texas, the real estate is going to sink into the ocean." What made Oldenburg unique is that, not only was he presenting the loan package but he was also the appraiser. "He knew he would get a commission if the loan was made," says Anderson, "So when they asked him, 'are you sure it's a good loan?' 'Of course', he said, 'it's a good loan'. And of course it was a con job."

"This little Savings and Loan was lending money to families, fourplexes, apartments, duplexes, and homes in their immediate market," says Anderson. "But Henry was the sponsor of the first out-of-state loan to a Texas-based condominium developer with a character like Oldenburg."

Hyde in Starr Country

Clyde's failed condo deal with Oldenburg plunged the Judiciary Chairman deep into Arkansas and right into the middle of Ken Starr's $50 million Whitewater inquiry. "It is extremely likely that Starr learned a great deal about Henry's risky dealings," says Anderson, "because the Rose Law Firm with Hillary Clinton, Wes Hubel and Vince Forster was hired by the federal government to litigate Guaranty, where Clyde, at the direction of Henry, had gone into business with Oldenburg."

Anderson's statement is well documented in press accounts and in *Bloodsport* by James Stewart. The Rose Law Firm, like many private legal firms during the height of the massive bailout, was hired by federal regulators in 1995 to litigate the $82 million bailout of Guaranty. "This means Ken Starr, who was tracking every move Hillary made, would have easily stumbled on Henry's shady deals with Oldenburg and Swink."

In fact, a key aspect of the Fed's $17.2 million civil suit against Clyde's board focuses on the Arkansas connection. The Feds cited Clyde for gross negligence in the Oldenburg condo project, stating that the board "failed to establish any appropriate written loan policies, procedures or guidelines governing out-of-state construction lending, and the Arkansas Princess loan was made without the benefit of any such policies, procedures or guidelines."

In August 1996, the *Illinois Legal Times* published a provocative expose detailing Hyde's actions at Clyde. The article points out several crucial omissions on a complex Whitewater flow chart put out in 1994 by Henry Hyde as Chairman of the Republican Policy Committee.

"The 'Whitewater Family' Tree was released under the name of the only sitting member of Congress to have been sued on a S&L-related charge," it wryly notes. The article goes on to point out that Hillary Clinton and the Rose Law Firm had been hired by the feds to litigate the Guaranty bailout, and also that Hillary Clinton and Clyde Federal were both invested in the same shady options trading company, Refco.

"A newly drawn Whitewater diagram should by rights include Guaranty Savings and Loan, as well as Refco," states the article, "but for Republicans, that would herald an ominous turn: a metastasis of the investigation. With Refco and Guaranty S&L on the diagram, one would have to draw a line all the way to North Riverside, Ill., and the name at its terminus would be Illinois Congressman Henry J. Hyde."

"If the independent counsel's mission was to leave no stone unturned in connection to failed S&L's in Arkansas that may have been connected to the Whitewater," says Anderson, "why wasn't Starr looking at Henry's relationship to both Swink and Oldenburg at Guaranty? The answer is simple: He'd end up having to pay a visit to one of the most powerful Republicans in the country, who also happened to be the head of the Judiciary Committee and the man in charge of evaluating Starr's case for impeachment," Anderson asserts. "Starr has obviously compromised his investigation by not following the obvious trails into Illinois."

A Very "Special" Deal for Henry

Henry Hyde is the Houdini of great S&L rip-off escapes. Hyde's successful effort to escape personal sanctions for his actions as a Clyde board member is the tale of a politician who demanded and received special treatment after committing gross violations of the public trust. "No man is above the law," was just not good enough when Hyde was the man.

As lead impeachment prosecutor, Hyde told Senators that the motion to dismiss by Robert Byrd was "a legal way of saying 'so what' to the charges" and would in essence brush off criminality. "Now a trial, as I understand it, is a search for truth," said Hyde indignantly, "and it should not be trumped by a search for an exit strategy. It seems to me this motion elevates convenience over constitutional process."

But Hyde's fierce belief in truth-searching trials was nowhere in sight when it came to his legal problems at Clyde.

In early 1997, more than six years after the Fed seized Clyde, and four years after Hyde and the others had been named in the $17.2 million lawsuit, the FDIC settled with the Clyde defendants for $850,000. The settlement for only 5 percent of the original amount asked for by the RTC was barely enough to cover the government's legal expenses during the long delays instigated by Hyde and the other defendants, and came nowhere near the losses of $67 million suffered by the taxpayers.

It was a good deal for the defendants for many reasons. The FDIC settled the case without undertaking any pretrial discovery, which could have opened the door to potentially damaging revelations about Clyde's dubious deals with men like Swink and Oldenburg. Furthermore, nobody admitted responsibility.

"I'm a victim of a lawsuit that never should have been brought," Hyde fumed after he was named in the RTC suit. "I'm not paying a nickel." After years of legal maneuvering, Henry Hyde was granted a special deal. Despite the fact that all eleven of his co-defendants on the board of Clyde were forced to pay nearly $1 million between them, Hyde paid the princely sum of—nothing. It was the remaining eleven board members who had to pick up his part of the $850,000 tab.

Hyde's special deal allowed him to separate himself from the other defendants and play up his role as the innocent victim of abusive government regulations. On November 19, 1996, Chairman Hyde released a written statement regarding the Clyde settlement. Hyde didn't hesitate to shift the blame and again deny responsibility. "It appears that the lawsuit will be dismissed as a result of negotiations among parties other than myself," proclaimed Hyde in his 1996 statement. "I have not agreed to, nor will I agree, to make any payment in settlement of this case...In participating in the business of the board, I relied, when appropriate, on the expertise of professionals in the field and full-time officers and employees...and thus was guilty of no negligence much less gross negligence as charged in the lawsuit."

Walker Todd is the former assistant general counsel and research officer for the Federal Reserve Bank of Cleveland. Todd believes that politics influenced the decision to spare Hyde from the financial fallout of Clyde's $67 million collapse. "If his name was John Q. Public, it's obvious he would never escape," said Todd, an economist who oversaw loans to troubled S&Ls. "If you were ranking the directors by guilt or responsibility or negligence, Hyde might have made the top four or five. If you were one of the [eleven] directors in that chain, you'd wonder why you're paying and he's not."

Lawyers for other defendants told *The New York Times* "they had no choice but to go along with Hyde's refusal to contribute." Sean Sullivan, a Chicago lawyer who represented several former Clyde board members told the *Times* after the settlement: "The others have long since gotten over their irritation that Henry insists on paying nothing...for the others in the Clyde mess," said Sullivan. "It's just too expensive to take the case to trial."

A former member of Clyde's board, who asked not to be named, confronted the issue of fairness head-on. He said he believed it was "pretty clear...a reasonable surmise" that Hyde's political prominence spared the House Judiciary Committee chairman from paying his share of the $850,000. Hyde, he said, escaped having to pay because of his position in Congress, not because he was any less guilty than the rest. While the former member said he felt no personal animosity or ill will toward the Chairman, he didn't think it was exactly fair. "No, of course I didn't. Obviously I think we should have all paid and I don't know how he got away with it," says the former Clyde board member. "I understood that if I tried to do it the way he did I would still be in court fighting. If I had played that game they would have taken me to court and that is very expensive." Unlike Hyde, who was quite well off, says the former board member, "there were a couple of people who were retired; it was tough, really tough for them."

"The gross negligence case against the twelve members of Clyde's board has withstood substantial scrutiny," Ruskin pointed out in his letter to the FDIC chairman, asking for the case to be reopened. On behalf of CAP, Ruskin wanted to know "why the FDIC proposed to settle the Clyde case without undertaking thorough pretrial discovery? Why is the FDIC confident that it has all of the materials in its possession necessary for a review for all possible civil and criminal liability in the case? Taxpayers deserve to know why the FDIC apparently will not require all of Clyde's directors to pay at least some amount to the FDIC. Should we conclude," Ruskin asks, "that the FDIC is rolling over and playing dead? If so, then what does that say about the health and fairness of our civil justice system which Chairman Hyde oversees? Has Hyde used his position as Chairman of the House Judiciary Committee to escape payment in the civil suit against him and Clyde's other directors?"

In response to queries from the Congressional Accountability Project, the FDIC candidly admitted giving Hyde a special deal. "It's totally immaterial to us," said a spokesman for the agency. "As long we're getting all the money we think is appropriate, we try to accommodate some individual, special requests."

Does it really matter that Hyde gets away with paying nothing, as long as someone foots the bill?

Hyde's special treatment, wrote Ralph Nader in March 1997, sets a dangerous precedent and could have a devastating impact on the stability of the federally insured banking system. Nader has characterized the wild S&L feeding frenzy that resulted from deregulation legislation as "the most outrageous example of banking corruption and governmental deregulatory complicity in American history." Nader said the deal sent a dangerous message to those who would become the future stewards of America's federally insured banking institutions.

"The settlement in the Illinois case raises new suspicions about how the system works," Nader stated. "To begin with, the $850,000 settlement is meager when tax-payers lost $67 million—not exactly a powerful message to send to governing boards of nation's insured financial institutions. The story gets worse," Nadar continued, "when the most illustrious and most influential member of the board of directors walks without contributing to even this small settlement...If the FDIC lets directors like Congressman Hyde walk away from a court settlement, the agency sets a dangerous policy that not only smacks of favoritism, but takes the heart out of the concept of cor-porate governance that says all directors—outside as well as inside—share in the fiduciary responsibility."

"A by-product of the civil actions," Nadar points out, should be "a strengthening of the 'first line of defense' represented by corporate boards of directors of financial institutions. Without directors willing to step up to their responsibility, the federal government's deposit insurance funds and the nation's taxpayers are in peril, new laws and regulations notwithstanding."

The special deal given Hyde by the FDIC flies in the face of the FDIC's own policy statement before the 104th Congress. At that time the FDIC was supporting stronger regulations for the industry and more liability for those in control of federally insured funds. "All directors of insured depository institutions, regardless of whether they are inside or outside directors, have a duty to set policies of their institutions and see that those policies are implemented and adhered to while meeting its community needs on a safe and sound basis, "the FDIC told Congress. "We believe good corporate gover-nance and effective regulatory oversight require that all directors know that they will be held responsible for ful-filling their duties to properly manage their institution.

Put differently, telling outside directors that they can be negligent with impunity is definitely the wrong message."

If even the FDIC agrees in holding board members responsible, why was Hyde treated with kid gloves? Ed Kane is the Cleary Professor of Finance at Boston College, and has written extensively on the key role played by Congress in the S&L meltdown. He argues that it was a disservice that the Chairman's case was never resolved through an in-depth investigation. He says he is puzzled as to why a special prosecutor was not appointed in the Clyde case, which raised many serious questions of "conflict of interest and influence pedaling" and "where taxpayers lost so much money. There was so much prima facie evidence of conflict of interest," Kane says, "it really stands out to me that the independent counsel statute wasn't used in this case."

If there's not clear investigation and swift enforcement, says the distinguished college professor, there is little incentive for future board members to act in the public's best interest. "If someone may have done wrong in violating the public trust, what obligations will other public servants have to clarify what went wrong, and to punish the person who violated this trust? Here you're left not knowing how the evidence was sorted out."

Kane says Hyde's role as a board director at Clyde would almost necessarily conflict with his duties as a member of Congress and a representative of the people. "Any director owes duties of loyalty to the stockholders and other stakeholders in an institution that has employed or appointed him," says Kane. "At the same time every member of Congress owes a duty of loyalty to taxpayers. So these are duties of loyalty and care that conflict completely because of the fact that most things that help the taxpayer would reduce returns to some of the stakeholders in the S&L and many things that would increase returns to the stakeholders in the S&L would hurt taxpayers."

Kane's point was driven home in real terms in May 1989 when Hyde, as a member of the House Judiciary Committee, voted to put his own self-interest before the taxpayers by introducing legislation that would further weaken capitalization standards for troubled S&Ls, and risk increasing the cost of the bailout by billions. According to the *American Banker*, Hyde's "goodwill" amendment to the bailout legislation "could have prevented regulators from taking action for a year or more against an estimated 450 thrifts" including Clyde. As the *New Republic* noted in January 1995, if Hyde had been successful, "Clyde might have been able to stay open longer, concealing the negligence and mismanagement" that devastated the sleepy Illinois S&L.

After years of S&L nightmare stories, Hyde's amendment received little support among his colleagues and even less in the press. In May of 1989, the *Los Angeles Times* reported that Hyde's risky pro-industry amendment "would invite a whole new cycle of financial failures and bankruptcies." *Washington Post* editorial writers characterized the Hyde legislation as a "fig leaf invented to hide the financial nakedness of many S&Ls." The *New York Times* reported on June 16, 1989 that "the Hyde amendment would have given hundreds of savings associations with very little net worth a potentially lengthy appeals process before regulators could impose disciplinary measures." Even President George Bush opposed Hyde's measure, but opposition from his own party's president did not dampen Hyde's determined support of industry sought legislation. Ironically, Hyde's amendment was defeated 326 to ninety-four on the same day Congress voted to establish special offices to prosecute S&L fraud, as well as to establish civil penalties of up to $1 million a day for specific S&L crimes and to forbid further investments in junk bonds.

Tim Anderson is a bit less subtle than Professor Kane. The whistle blower from Libertyville says Hyde's dual role presented a potential conflict of interest that should have shown up like the Grand Canyon on a road map. Anderson was also concerned about the potential for conflict of interest and the abuse of the public trust when a powerful elected official such as Hyde controlled the purse strings of a federally insured institution. "Every loan approved while Hyde was on the board," said Anderson, "should have been reviewed to see if it had been approved for political consideration...You cannot be an elected official and the godfather of the vault at the same time."

In light of his relentless effort to impeach and then oust President Clinton for obstruction of justice, Hyde's efforts on Clyde's behalf take on a deep hue of irony. Anderson says Hyde "fought viciously for regulators to allow thrifts to stay open longer so they could try to work their way out of debt." But, "he had a conflict of interest," says Anderson. "It was his thrift, Clyde Federal, he was trying to keep open. So why is this congressman making a motion to keep open a thrift that he has been a director of? Was the Chairman of the Judiciary, the man now at the center of the entire impeachment process, trying to prevent or distract an eventual lawsuit?"

Political Muscle Restrains the Feds

Tim Anderson offers a very compelling theory for why Illinois became "ground zero" for the S&L melt-down. And it has everything to do with lobbyists, and three powerful Illinois Republicans, including Henry Hyde.

In Illinois, deregulation took on a special meaning, for it was the home of the U.S. League of Savings and Loans, the industry's powerful lobbying arm. As thrift deregulation was starting to take its toll, the U.S. League was pressing hard for legislation that would help keep the lid on the burgeoning crisis. The industry used a prominent trio of Republicans, says Anderson, to help push their legislation through Congress, and as "front-line protection to insulate them" from regulatory and legal scrutiny.

All three Republicans sat on boards of failed S&Ls in the 1980s: House Judiciary Chairman and later chief impeachment prosecutor, Henry Hyde; former Congressman and Bush Secretary of Agriculture, Edward Madigan; and former Congressman and Bush Administration Secretary of Veterans Affairs, Edwin Derwinski. "The U.S. League knew that if they had Madigan, Henry Hyde and Derwinski on bank boards in the state, that would give them extra protection. None of the government agencies could investigate Illinois because they would trip over Congressman Henry Hyde," and other prominent board members.

The strategy apparently worked. Key S&Ls in Illinois with prominent Republicans on their boards were able to continue operating after many others around the nation were shut down. "It was like taking a cruise on the Titanic after it started to sink," says Anderson. The extra time given to the Illinois S&L's both delayed the bad news of the impending disaster and increased the ultimate cost of the bailout by billions. "Henry's importance in this is his direct involvement," says Anderson. "There was the extraordinary latitude given to the Illinois S&L," continues Anderson. "Scratch the surface on some of these operations and you can begin to see the pattern of special deals, endless delays, and kid-glove handling."

Elaine Hopkins of the *Peoria-Journal Star*, a Peoria Illinois-based daily, was one of the few mainstream reporters to latch on to the S&L story in the land of Lincoln. Starting in 1992, Hopkins began trying to pry the lid of the Illinois/S&L connection and find out how "$3.5 billion disappeared from over a hundred S&Ls" in her home state. "Answers are hard to get because Illinois S&L records are stored in boxes in a Kansas City warehouse," wrote Hopkins in January 1994. "Someone in Washington decided to close the Illinois office and ship out the records, a perfect way to bury what happened... What I learned about Illinois S&Ls raises many questions that need answers. The most important: whether three highly placed Illinois Republicans used their clout to influence the S&L situation...Demands from politicians in Congress for a thorough investigation into the Arkansas S&L where the Clintons had high-placed friends should make Illinois residents laugh. Or cry," stated Hopkins.

Tim Anderson was certainly not laughing in February 1993 when he was called to testify before the National Commission on Financial Institution Reform, Recovery and Enforcement. The commission was investigating various aspects of the S&L crisis under special statutes of the 1986 anti-crime bill. In sworn testimony before the commission, Anderson criticized federal prosecutors for failing to press forward with Clyde and other Illinois S&L failures. "They don't want to do it because the conclusion will come back to very prominent people," Anderson said.

Anderson singled out for special criticism U.S. Attorney Fred Forman, a politically ambitious Republican who handled federal prosecutions in Chicago from 1990 to 1993. "Fred Forman's dilemma is, if he starts investigating seriously the failed Savings and Loans in Illinois, he will see they all link together," Anderson testified. "Then, he might have to start taking depositions from now former Cabinet member Ed Madigan, former Cabinet member Ed Derwinski, and current Congressman Henry Hyde. And Fred Forman just isn't brave enough to start taking depositions from these individuals. So Illinois is going to be buried."

Forman's record regarding criminal prosecutions of S&L cases is less than impressive. National statistics regarding prosecution in other states show that criminal fraud was a common offense in S&L failures from coast to coast. As much as 60 percent and more of S&L cases involved some form of criminal activity. Forman's track record was only one-fourth the national recorded average. Tim Anderson asserts that Forman's resistance was directly related to the fact that Hyde and several other powerful Republicans were on the boards of troubled S&Ls.

Gary Ruskin of CAP also questioned the low number of prosecutions in Illinois. "Clyde falls into a curious pattern of unusually low levels of prosecutorial activity in Illinois RTC cases. Illinois had the lowest prosecution rate of any of the twenty-two states with over ten RTC thrifts."

This, says Ruskin, supports allegations from critics like Tim Anderson of "prosecutorial lassitude in cases against Illinois Savings and Loan directors...The American people deserve a full and thorough explanation of why this pattern exists in Illinois, and what might be done to remedy it."

Former Resolution Trust investigator, Fred Cedarholm, doesn't lay all the blame at the heels of Forman or any one prosecutor. He says it is quite feasible that Forman never saw the dozens of criminal referrals churned out by Cedarholm and colleagues at the RTC's bustling Chicago office before it was abruptly shut down.

But Cedarholm did express deep concern about the immense political pressure placed on prosecutors assigned to investigate the S&Ls. In fact, he said that the RTC investigations of Clyde and other well-connected Illinois S&Ls faced political sabotage in 1992 when the Bush administration shut down the RTC office in Chicago and moved many key investigations to Kansas City "for strictly political reasons."

As a former federal investigator for RTC, Cedarholm carried out detailed audits on hundreds of million of dollars in bank loans, specifically evaluating director and officer liabilities. He says closing down the office in Chicago, the largest in the country, "most definitely" crippled key government investigations and cost taxpayers tens of millions in additional costs. "Based on dirt we'd uncovered," said Cedarholm, "there is no way in hell the Chicago office should have been shut down. It was done for strictly political reasons...They really did pull the rug out from under us. We were doing a lot of squeezing, not only of the executives and the board members, but actually bringing in the borrowers...and deposing them, and they were starting to sweat. We were turning up a lot of good stuff which I'm sure was creating a lot of waves in Washington D.C. When you consider the number of cases we had, the depth of those cases and the potential liabilities, it was basically ridiculous to take cases from the people who had been working on them for years in Chicago and give them to people in Kansas City to start all over."

According to Cedarholm, there are "two very good reasons" why Illinois did not receive intense public scrutiny the way Texas and California did, and was thus spared the harsh spotlight of negative publicity. "First, it was the home of the United States League of Savings Institutions," the most powerful lobby group for S&Ls. "Secondly, it had some of the most powerful politicians in the country" sitting on the boards of its newly deregulated S&Ls. "As far as I know, Illinois had the only two S&Ls that had direct ties to Congressmen," said Cedarholm. "Henry Hyde was the only Congressman, nationwide, who was a director of an S&L and Ed Madigan, a former U.S. Congressman, was a director of Olympic, a mile or so down the road from Clyde. So we have the only two S&Ls in the country tied to Congressmen both of whom are Republicans located in Illinois."

A July 1992 article in the *National Law Journal* backs up Cedarholm's assertions of a Bush political purge at RTC. The respected legal newspaper reported that according to "one inside attorney" the shake-up was a "gross election-year interference by the White House" because "so many targets" of RTC lawsuits and investigations were turning out to be "prominent individuals with strong Republican ties." The "purge" left Edward Stephenson, assistant director of the Government Accountability Office, scratching his head in wonder. "You had the attorneys in the field doing a heck of a job," said Stephenson, "filing a bunch of lawsuits under terrible time constraints…They were going out and getting the job done. What was the basis for their removal?"

While Cedarholm played no direct role in the investigation at Clyde, he did recall some of the details of the case. He finds Hyde's current talk of cooperation on the impeachment issue ironic. "Most of the directors were fairly cooperative in that situation, as I remember, but Hyde never provided a thing. His attitude was basically that 'I'm a U.S. Congressman. I've done nothing wrong. End of discussion.' Now to have him at the Judiciary pontificating is just amazing."

Rushing to Hyde's Defense

Apparently, it wasn't enough that he escaped all financial responsibility in the FDIC/Clyde settlement. On January 8, 1997, over three years after he was named in the $17.2 million-dollar Clyde suit, Hyde filed papers with the State of Illinois for a defense fund to pick up the tab for his protracted legal battles. The Judiciary Chairman had spent more than three years trying to stave off federal investigators. "I am paying debts in the legitimate defense of a lawsuit that was an abuse of governmental power," Hyde told *The Chicago Sun Times*. "This is a device for collecting the money so my lawyer doesn't hold the bag. I don't have a checking account. I am living on my monthly salary."

Even more interesting than the defense fund itself are the people who created the Henry J. Hyde Defense Fund Trust. At the center is Jeremiah Marsh. Marsh was the Chairman of the Board of Hopkins and Sutter, a well-connected law firm with offices in Chicago and Washington D.C. Hopkins & Sutter hauled in tens of millions in legal fees related to the S&L bailout.

An April 1997 issue of *Cranes Business Weekly* reported that Hopkins & Sutter "prospered from the implosion of the Savings and Loan Industry." It noted that "the influential Chicago law firm raked in over $20 million in taxpayer-supplied fees annually, ranking No. 1 nationally, in clean-up fees from the S&L crash." Hopkins & Sutter and other law firms were eventually reigned in by Congress, when some angry lawmakers slapped a $2.5 million cap on what any one firm could make on the bailout. "I'd say that Hopkins & Sutter owe quite a debt of gratitude to the likes of Henry Hyde and the others," quipped Tim Anderson. "It was their kind of flagrant abuse of civil banking practices and federal regulations" that left taxpayers with a $200 billion bailout bill.

In an April 9, 1997, letter to invited members of the Hyde defense committee, Marsh informed them about the good news of Hyde's victory. House Judiciary Chairman Henry Hyde "has been engaged for many months in litigation that has just recently been settled. I have enclosed a clipping which tells as much of the story as is necessary to know. The Chairman never wavered from his position that he was not responsible for the institution's losses, and he was successful. The case is over."

Then Marsh, like any good fundraiser, hit with the bad news and the pitch. "Unfortunately the legal fees are not over and that is the purpose of my letter. I am asking you to become a member of the Henry J. Hyde Defense Fund Trust which will hold its first meeting at 6:30 p.m. at the Georgetown Club Restaurant in Washington D.C. on Monday April 14, 1997."

According to the invitation, if all went well and everybody showed up at the dinner with $2,500, the newly formed defense committee could put itself out of business after the first meeting. In his letter, Marsh was quite specific about who could contribute to the fund, which included political PACs, corporations and nearly everyone else except lobbyists. "But their family members and employers may," according to Jeremiah Marsh.

Hyde told reporters at the time of the settlement, "I was always prepared to go to trial no matter what the cost. I was determined not to surrender to a claim that was without foundation and, in my opinion, an abuse of government power."

Among Hyde's good friends who stepped forward with checks, kind words and moral support was Thomas Smeeton, who worked under Hyde as chief investigator for the House Judiciary Committee before retiring in 1996. Smeeton gladly assumed the role as trustee for Hyde's defense fund. Others who contributed were Walter Malinowski, president and CEO of Labat Anderson, which makes its money from government contracts. Malinowski, a big Republican contributor, kicked in $2,000 for Hyde's legal bills. Another prominent contributor was Zachary Fisher of NYC, a wealthy real estate developer, who gave Hyde $5,000.

"The knowledge that he wouldn't have to cough up much, if any, of that legal bill," stated a *Crane's Business News Service* article, "explains Mr. Hyde's hard-line stance against a federal lawsuit alleging director negligence. None of twelve directors admitted blame when the lawsuit was settled last month, yet Mr. Hyde alone refused to chip in to cover $850,000 in settlement costs." But then, with the outstanding service he provided to the financial industry, it's little surprise that he, and only he of the twelve board members, could count on friends in high places to pay his legal tab.

Enter Henry Hyde's Worst Nightmare

Tim Anderson, in addition to being a former Marine, has been many things in his life, including a razor salesman, and a manufacturer of his own brand of suntan oil. He is a well-known member of his church. His crusade "to hold Hyde and the other S&L crooks accountable" has cost him his business and nearly his family. He has spent the last decade investigating Henry Hyde, and a host of other politicians, lobbyists, industry-controlled regulators, reluctant prosecutors, and S&L crooks. Anderson says they all went absolutely wild when the gates of deregulation were thrown open.

Anderson ran a modest bank consulting firm through the 1980s that was netting him a comfortable living. "It was through my work that I started to notice how many of the thrifts in our local Illinois area were becoming insolvent," said Anderson, during an interview. "I became curious when my hometown S&L in Libertyville, Illinois was becoming insolvent. My mother kept her CDs there. It got me scratching my head, wondering why my hometown S&L would become insolvent when I lived in a flourishing and very prosperous neighborhood."

Over the next dozen years, Anderson did a lot more than scratch his head and wonder. He gave up his consulting business, took on a less demanding job moving cars for a rental agency, and zeroed in on Henry Hyde's role at Clyde. He has now become Hyde's worst nightmare: a one-man truth squad on the shady dealings at Clyde.

Armed with his own knowledge, a network of associates in the banking industry trenches, and the Freedom of Information Act, Anderson has managed to keep the Clyde case alive. "It's clear Henry's not single-handedly responsible for the entire S&L fiasco," said Anderson, "but he's a real good place to start looking, especially now that he is busy prosecuting the President of the United states for violating the public's trust."

Henry's Gumshoe

"I didn't hire him. I didn't pay him. I didn't direct him."
> —Hyde speaking about Private Investigator
> Ernie Rizzo, October 18, 1998

David Kendall's questioning of Kenneth Starr before the House Judiciary Committee was proceeding smoothly towards its conclusion on November 19, 1998. But it didn't last long after Kendall asked Starr whether he hired private investigators to interview women in Little Rock, and followed by asking Starr about his spending "half-a-million dollars for, among other things, private investigators."

A sudden interruption by Chairman Henry Hyde brought the line of inquiry to a halt before any audit report on private investigators could be discussed. "Well, the Chair has got to intervene. The hour is over," interjected Hyde. And that was the end. "I'm simply trying to get my fair crack at him," implored Kendall, but to no avail. Hyde moved on to recognize Republican counsel David Schippers for thirty minutes.

Many listening to the proceedings were unaware of a *Chicago Tribune* editorial published on the very same morning of the hearings, which might have unnerved Hyde enough to cut off Kendall. As mentioned earlier, the *Chicago Tribune* was echoing an October 26 call by the Congressional Accountability Project. They both called for the House Ethics Committee to explore the circumstances of a man hired by Hyde's attorney to investigate Tim Anderson: the well-known private eye, Ernie Rizzo. Rizzo has provided services for OJ Simpson and many Hollywood stars.

Hyde understands well the ethical problems of a powerful government official hiring a gumshoe to spy on a private citizen. Two weeks before the editorial, in his eighty-one written questions, Hyde asked Clinton about "the past or present direct or indirect employment of individuals, other than counsel representing you, whose duties include making contact with or gathering information about witnesses or potential witnesses in any judicial proceeding related to any matter in which you are or could be involved."

The situations could not be more parallel. Through his attorney and friend, James Schirott, Hyde had hired his own gumshoe in 1995 to investigate someone who would certainly be a star "potential witness" if there ever were to be "any judicial proceeding related to any matter" involving Henry Hyde. But in Hyde's moral universe, the application of ethical standards depends on who you are.

A Bandit on the Bank Board

Going Undercover

On October 20, 1998, Chicago-based private-eye Ernie Rizzo acknowledged during a radio interview that he was hired to do "a total and complete investigation" of independent banking consultant Tim Anderson. The reason? "Apparently he was following a particular federal lawsuit a little too close. Some of the parties involved in the lawsuit wanted to know what his interest was," said Rizzo.

During his two-month undercover investigation, Rizzo posed as an independent TV producer doing research for a show about Anderson's story. According to Rizzo, this allowed him to interview "quite a few people" associated with Anderson, including "working people, neighbors, business associates, things like that." Rizzo even had one long meeting with Anderson in a restaurant. Believing Rizzo to be a television journalist, and eager to get his story out, Anderson provided Rizzo with 380 pages of documentation on Hyde's involvement in irresponsible investments that eventually brought down Clyde.

As Anderson later recounted, when he and Rizzo discussed Hyde's misadventures over a cheeseburger and fries, Rizzo "kept telling me what I didn't have. I kept asking him who he was a television producer for and what he had done in the past, but he avoided the questions."

In reaction to Anderson's exercise of his constitutional rights, Hyde's lawyer Schirott felt compelled to hire a high-priced investigator. What was so troubling to him? "No one knew who Anderson was," says Rizzo, or why he "kept appearing in court, why he kept appearing in the judge's chambers and [why] he wanted to see the Savings & Loan thing resolved...My client wanted to know what his position was, who he was, what he was doing in this case." Rizzo said that Anderson "apparently had a desperate need to see that the directors of the Clyde Savings & Loan were punished and he wasn't going to let go until they were punished."

Rizzo said he found Anderson to be exactly what he claimed to be: A concerned and well-informed citizen who was angry because Henry Hyde, one of the most powerful men in Congress, was never held accountable. According to Rizzo, Anderson spoke "fluently" and willingly provided Rizzo with nearly 400 pages of documents detailing the abuses by Hyde and the other board members. When Rizzo, with thirty years experience as a celebrated private investigator, was asked if he found anything that Anderson was saying to be made up, false, a bold face lie or misleading, he replied candidly, "No, not really."

Even so, Hyde spokesman Sam Stratman said that Anderson was making "malicious, arguably slanderous and libelous allegations against Mr. Hyde," and that's why Schirott's office hired the PI to spy on Anderson. "If I was libeling Hyde," says Anderson, "he should sue me in court, not have somebody pose as a journalist to investigate me."

In an October radio interview, Rizzo of course would not say who "his client" was. He would not confirm or deny that the man was Hyde. He said he made Anderson's documents and a report available to "just one person." Hyde claimed he was informed about the results of the investigation and received the report, but, he told *The Chicago Tribune*, "I didn't hire him. I didn't pay him. I didn't direct him." *The Tribune* also reported that Hyde denied that "anyone working under his direction hired the detective." Hyde said that the service was provided by a "mutual friend" and that he could not remember this friend's name.

Hyde's apparent lies and attempted cover-up began to fall apart when *Roll Call* reported that Rizzo said in an interview "that he did the job for Hyde and his lawyer and was paid with a cashier's check in the mail."

If Hyde received services from Rizzo that were paid for by someone else, he is required by law to report this as a gift to the House Ethics Committee. On October 26, the Congressional Accountability Project called for a formal ethics investigation into whether Henry Hyde "violated the House gift rule by receiving free investigative services from a private investigator, Ernie Rizzo." At that point, the amount paid to Rizzo was unknown. Rizzo still had not been permitted to disclose his fee, but said he is normally paid $10,000 for a comparable job.

When it became clear that if Hyde hadn't paid for the services he might therefore have a gift problem on his hands, Hyde changed his story. He admitted that his "friend" whose name he could not remember earlier was none other than his longtime personal attorney, James Schirott. To explain Hyde's previous denial that anyone working for him hired Rizzo, Hyde's spokesman said that Schirott hired Rizzo without Hyde's knowledge. Seeking to explain Hyde's inconsistencies, the spokesman said, "Mr. Hyde was asked about something that happened years ago and given only a moment's notice to respond. His immediate response was that a friend hired Mr. Rizzo. Mr. Schirott is a lawyer and a friend, and Mr. Hyde's response was correct."

But then Hyde's claim that he did not pay for the Anderson investigation fell apart, too. Spokesman

Stratman acknowledged that Hyde reimbursed Schirott for Rizzo's work. Schirott then said that he paid Rizzo $2,000 for his two-month investigation. Though other evidence has come to light suggesting it was, in fact, $10,000, Rizzo still will not confirm or deny the amount.

The Chairman of the House Judiciary Committee—who demanded "complete and specific" answers to his eighty-one questions from President Clinton—had at best given conflicting and incomplete explanations about his own use of a private eye. At worst, he outright lied and then changed his story when the heat was on.

In December, Hyde made a statement that certainly implies he knew about Schirott's hiring of Rizzo all along. "I didn't direct him what to do or how to do it," Hyde said of Rizzo. "I certainly didn't tell him to deceive anybody."

Meanwhile, Gary Ruskin, Director of the Congressional Accountability Project, has heard only silence in response to his October request for an Ethics Committee investigation into Henry Hyde. "They've made no written response to me. They've made no oral response to me," he said in February of 1999. "I usually know when there is a response and I think they're not doing anything. But I don't know if Henry Hyde has sent anything to the Ethics Committee."

Muzzling Rizzo

The Chicago radio program *News Talk 89*, with host Nancy Skinner, began its broadcast on January 30, 1999, with some startling news. That very day, station WLS had learned about the results of a new *Chicago Tribune* poll. It showed that 35 percent of the voters in Henry Hyde's district of DuPage County, which is staunchly

Republican, have been "turned off" by Hyde's performance as chief impeachment prosecutor and say they now have "a lower opinion of the veteran Congressman as a result."

Ironically, the station was scheduled to interview both Ernie Rizzo and Tim Anderson that day on the listener call-in, commercial radio program. The plan was to talk to the two guests about the published record. Nothing new or particularly exciting was anticipated on this winter Saturday afternoon. But what happened next shows Henry Hyde in the act of exercising raw power.

Skinner had talked to Rizzo the day before about receiving payment for the Anderson investigation. He told her on the record, she said, "that he had been paid $10,000 for his services by money order in December of 1995." She also had called Hyde's spokesperson, Sam Stratman, to invite him to join Rizzo and Anderson on the show. "Let's just say Stratman seemed none too pleased to learn of this development and they officially never returned my call," Skinner said.

Within an hour of that call, Skinner received a call from Rizzo saying "a big fish in Chicago" contacted him who was "fuming mad" and told him that "he would never work again if he went on the show." In a later call the same day, Rizzo told Skinner that Edward Vrdolyak—a prominent lawyer and major GOP powerbroker—had been hired by Henry Hyde to stop his appearance on the show. Rizzo played a clip of Vrdolyak's message on his answering machine—whose voice Skinner recognized because he used to have a talk show on WLS—which said something like "as time progresses you'll know you've done the right thing." Rizzo told Skinner that the threat that he would never work again had come straight from Hyde. Rizzo then faxed her a letter on Vrdolyak's legal stationary advising Skinner that "under the advice of counsel, Ernie Rizzo will not be participating in your radio show" because it might violate confidentiality between Rizzo and "his client."

The letter from Vrdolyak was signed on his behalf by Paul A. Karkula, another attorney with his firm. A few days later, in an interview, Karkula said he did not know if Hyde was a client of the firm. He did not return the call to clarify that as promised. Rizzo, also in a follow-up interview, suggested at first that Nancy Skinner exaggerated aspects of the story. Rather than threatening him with never working again, Rizzo said that Vrdolyak "helped clarify my responsibilities under the law." However, he confirmed his interactions with Skinner and would not deny any of the key points that Skinner made on the air, including the delivery of the $10,000 money order.

Skinner then received a third call from Rizzo. "I learned that this panic attack went from the U.S. Capitol to the State Capitol and to Chicago," she said, "and that very powerful political figures in Illinois advised Rizzo that he should not go on our show."

Skinner told the whole story on the air, noting, "This was supposed to be a little weekend talk show about previously published information in the *Trib* and elsewhere. And Congressman Hyde's office is on def con five. That's the story. I think he doth protest too much."

As of this writing, the secrecy shrouding the Rizzo matter has not let up. Even though the Congressional Accountability Project is still calling for an ethics investigation into Hyde, his attorney Schirott has refused to provide answers to the nagging questions: who paid for

Rizzo, how much was he paid, and will he be released from confidentiality to talk to reporters? Independent faxes to Schirott from a *Chicago Tribune* reporter and these writers on March 10 and 11—requesting proof that will resolve the issue once and for all—received no response. Yet at the same time, Hyde was still adamantly denying his own role in the Rizzo affair: "I never hired a private investigator to look into the background of any individual," he proclaimed in a March 10 letter to the *Tribune*.

And in another bizarre twist, Rizzo suddenly flip-flopped on March 5 and said that Vrdolyak was his lawyer, after previously denying it numerous times. The next step in the saga is anybody's guess.

Chapter 4

Man of Zeal

The Rule of Law vs. the Rule of Henry Hyde

"Truth telling, truth telling, is the heart and soul of our justice system. I think the answer would have been clear to those who once pledged their sacred honor to the cause of liberty. The answer would have been clear to those who crafted the world's most enduring written constitution."
—Henry Hyde, January 16, 1999

"We have all been sermonized about how terrible lying is, and that is a given. I certainly accept that. But 'the end doesn't justify the means'—it just seems to me is too simplistic when you have to deal with some very difficult, complex moral situations..."
—Henry Hyde, July 17, 1987

During the impeachment proceedings in 1998, Chairman Hyde claimed to be fighting to "preserve the rule of law," against such acts as perjury and obstruction of justice. But during the hearings into the Iran-Contra scandal in 1987, he vigorously argued against the importance of the rule of law. And he did so even when breaking the law was far more serious in this case. Indeed, as Peter Kornbluh, a senior analyst at the National Security Archives in Washington D.C. and a widely respected expert on the Iran-Contra affair, explains the scandal, it was "a flagrant and deliberate effort to violate, circumvent and ignore explicit Congressional law. The Iran-Contra operations were a rape of the pillar of the Constitution and its checks and balances."

But subverting the will of Congress didn't bother Henry Hyde. "All of us at some time confront conflicts between rights and duties," Hyde reflected, "between choices that are evil and less evil, and one hardly exhausts moral imagination by labeling every untruth and every deception an outrage." Hyde evoked the spirit of Jefferson to make his point and defend his cherished compatriot, Oliver North: "…A strict adherence to the written law is doubtless one of the highest duties of a good citizen, but it is not the highest…On great occasions every good officer must be ready to risk himself in going beyond the strict line of [the] law."

"Almost every single word Hyde uttered" during impeachment proceedings, says Peter Kornbluh of the National Security Archives, "could be turned around and used against him. The law wasn't so principled and straightforward back then for Hyde…it was as malleable as he wanted it to be…" A critical example of that malleability concerns Hyde's reaction to the Boland Amendment. As it was passed for fiscal year 1985, the amendment was crystal clear: It prohibited any expenditure of funds by the CIA or the Pentagon "or any other agency or entity of the United States involved in intelligence activities" for supporting, "directly or indirectly, military or paramilitary operations in Nicaragua by any nation, organization, group, or individual."

Boland was passed to prevent a war from breaking out between Nicaragua and Honduras. Honduras had become the home of the Contra's northern front and a major staging area for Contra attacks against the Nicaraguan Sandinista government. The tensions between the two countries were high because of the CIA/Contra presence. Boland was also expanded as a result of systematic and widespread human rights violations by Contra forces, a point to which we will return.

Hyde's response to the Boland Amendments was characteristically cavalier. "I know the Boland Amendment is damned important. I know that, any of the three versions, if you can understand it," mocked Hyde in 1987.

Indeed, destroying the credibility of the Boland Amendments was at the heart of the Republican strategy for derailing the Iran-Contra investigation, and Hyde, using all of his rhetorical skills, led the charge to discredit it. Throughout the duration of the hearings, Hyde repeatedly made the case that the Boland Amendments perhaps didn't cover the National Security Council, where Oliver North worked and managed the day-to-day operations of the secret Contra war. As North's loyal secretary, Fawn Hall, would proudly tell Congress, in defense of her boss, "Sometimes you have to go above the written law."

To circumvent the Boland Amendments, the Reagan administration created a "shadow CIA" operation that was moved into the National Security Council (NSC). Administration officials and "Congressional Contras," such as Hyde, would essentially pretend that Boland didn't cover the NSC because the NSC was not really an intelligence agency. The "shadow" covert operation would be supervised by North and other high-level administration officials. According to former NSC advisor, Admiral John Poindexter, North became the "switching point that made the whole system work." Lifelong Republican and Iran-Contra Special Counsel, Judge Lawrence Walsh stated that, through North and the NSC, "The CIA had continued as the agency overseeing U.S. undercover activities in support of the Contras after the Boland Amendments were enacted." According to Walsh, "The CIA's strategy determined what North would do." North was, in spy parlance, a "cut-out" for the CIA. The plan for the covertly-run CIA war was conceived by the Director of Central Intelligence, William Casey. The initial plan was to support the Contras by requesting aid from third-party countries such as El Salvador, Taiwan, Chile, Guatemala, South Africa, Israel, Brunei, Panama and Saudi Arabia. Saudi Arabia was an old friend of the U.S. and had funded U.S. covert wars in Afghanistan and Angola. By 1984 the Saudis were sending $1 million a month to the Contras via secret Swiss bank accounts, as well as other covert accounts in the Cayman Islands. By 1986 the Saudis had donated $30 million to the Contra cause.

Even before the first Boland Amendment was passed, the CIA was planning a strategy to circumvent it. According to former Contra leader, Edgar Chamorro, the CIA "consistently stated that there were plenty of ways to circumvent a law, so that it was not necessary to pay attention to the Boland Amendment or other laws." Chamorro writes in *Packaging the Contras: A Case of CIA Disinformation* that "Congress was viewed with blatant disrespect by the CIA because most members of Congress failed to understand the importance of covert actions. The Contras, and the war against Nicaragua, were 'too important' to be decided by a public debate or by elected officials. Those who knew better had to act decisively and educate the less-informed. In matters of anti-Communism, any means were justified in order to achieve victory. What was important was to win at all costs...The CIA bestowed on itself the mandate to decide the goals and priorities of the country's foreign policy, and to implement those goals covertly."

Mr. Bumble Takes a Tumble

How could Hyde, or any of the principal players, claim that the Boland Amendment didn't apply to the NSC when it clearly states that it covers the CIA, the Pentagon, and "any other agency or entity of the United States involved in intelligence activities?" Hyde predicated his professed confusion about whether the Boland Amendment covered the activities of the National Security Council in a confidential inquiry to an inexperienced thirty-three-year-old White House lawyer named Bretton Sciaroni.

In August 1985, Sciaroni was the sole professional staff member of Reagan's Intelligence Oversight Board. The board was responsible for reporting to the President whether any possible illegal activities were being conducted by intelligence agencies. Sciaroni was the administration's spokesperson on the issue of whether Boland applied to the NSC. Following numerous press reports alleging that Oliver North was engaged in illegal activities in aiding the Contras, Sciaroni prepared a legal opinion claiming that none of the Boland Amendments applied to the NSC.

Sciaroni's legal opinion on Boland was dismissed by the Iran-Contra Committee as laughable. Former Senator Warren Rudman, the Iran-Contra Committee's Republican vice-chairman, likened Sciaroni to Mr. Bumble, a Dickens character out of *Oliver Twist*, who has a penchant for exaggeration. Rudman characterized Sciaroni's opinion on Boland as an "outrageous, blatant attempt to subvert the law" by maintaining that the NSC was somehow not an "agency or entity of the United States involved in intelligence activities," as restricted under Boland. "I just want to tell you, Mr. Sciaroni, I think your opinion on that issue is just dead wrong."

Rudman was dead right when it came to Boland. No one doubted that the NSC was anything but an intelligence agency. According to Executive Order 12333, signed in December 1981, "The NSC shall act as the highest Executive Branch entity that provides review of, guidance for, and direction to the conduct of all national foreign intelligence, counterintelligence, and special activities and attendant policies and programs."

According to various sources, Sciaroni met with North a total of five minutes, with North denying that he had provided any military advice or financial assistance to the Contras. Sciaroni later briefly interviewed NSC Counsel Paul Thompson, who denied Sciaroni access to North's "working papers." Instead, Thompson gave him a one-inch thick stack of documents. Based on these documents and brief interviews with North and Thompson, Sciaroni issued his analysis.

According to Indepent Counsel Lawrence Walsh, "Sciaroni later admitted that he had been misled and that his legal opinion had been partially based on 'incorrect facts.' North blithely confessed that he had denied having engaged in fund-raising and having given military advice 'because after all, we viewed this to be a covert operation and he [Sciaroni] had absolutely no need to know the details of what I was doing.' Yet North apparently used Sciaroni's opinion to fend off questions about the legality of his actions."

To say he lacked the experience, expertise, and self-confidence to confront such heroic figures as Oliver North would clearly be an understatement. Sciaroni admitted during his congressional testimony that he had failed the bar examinations four times, including twice in California and twice in the District of Columbia, before finally passing in Pennsylvania. The young lawyer also admitted under questioning that his legal opinion on Boland, which Hyde held in such high esteem, was his first since graduating from law school.

No matter; Hyde was undeterred. He referred to the "morass of ambiguity as to what [Boland] means," while expressing his support for Sciaroni's discredited legal opinion. "Well, Mr. Sciaroni," stated Hyde, "we have conflicting opinions...on what the Boland Amendment means, and to whom it applies...I like your opinion so I want to talk to you about your opinion..."

Burning the Constitution to Save It:
An Owner's Manual

Does Hyde's defense of North really matter? After all, they were friends. But to focus solely on Hyde's efforts on North's behalf ignores the constitutional crisis created by the scandal—and Hyde's role in it. Lawrence Walsh characterized North as a zealot and a criminal who should have served time to set an example for future zealots in government who may be tempted to take the law into their own hands. "North prepared false documents for the purpose of obstructing Congressional investigations; he destroyed, altered and removed official documents; and he repeatedly participated in lying to Congress," says Walsh. "North seems to believe that such activities are business as usual in government or necessary tactics in a political firestorm."

But the more that was revealed about the North operation, and the extent of high-level Administration involvement, the more adamant Hyde's support became for the Iran-Contra law-breakers. Though Hyde threw a bone in the direction of his detractors, stating, "I do not wish to be understood as defending everything that was done by members of this Administration," he unabashedly defended the Reagan Administration to the end. His dissenting remarks to the majority report are nothing short of an attempt to blame Congress for the illegal policies implemented in secret by the Reagan Administration:

> We have had a disconcerting and distasteful whiff of moralism and institutional self-righteousness in these hearings. Too little have these committees acknowledged that the Executive may well have had the clearer vision of what was at stake in Central America. Too little have we acknowledged that our own convolutions have made the task of the Executive even more difficult...No one doubts that the Executive has done some very stupid things in this affair. But one would have liked to have seen some modest acknowledgment of

Congressional responsibility for our present policy impasse.

In 13 years of service in the House, it has seemed to me that Congress is usually more eager to assert authority than to accept responsibility; more ready to criticize rather than to constructively propose; more comfortable in the public relations limelight than in the murkier grayness of the real world, where choices must often be made, not between relative goods, but between bad and worse. These are not characteristics that give one confidence in Congress as a policy-making instrument for America's inescapable encounter with an often hostile world.

Kornbluh, co-author of *The Iran-Contra Scandal: The Classified History*, says he is "livid about the depth of Hyde's hypocrisy," revealed in his admonition of Clinton lying. Kornbluh says that, in contrast, the minority report on the Iran-Contra scandal championed by Hyde is "essentially a Congressional lie, a miswriting of history and a deliberate distortion…Hyde's dissenting views on the majority report were a clearcut effort to say lying is OK."

Even before much was understood as the scandal began unraveling in November of 1986, Hyde leapt to conclude that "there was no violation of the law," and that the U.S. policy of selling missiles to Iran was "unwise but not illegal." In a March 1985 letter to Max L. Friedersdorf of the White House Congressional Liaison Office, Robert McFarlane reports Hyde "felt that we should expand private-sector and third-country assistance, such as Taiwan and Saudi Arabia, in the effort to support the resistance."

Michael Ratner, co-founder of the Center for Constitutional Rights in New York City, says that Hyde's support for "third-country donations" to fight an illegal U.S. war is about as close as you can get "to outright starting a bonfire on the White House lawn" and burning the Constitution. "It is a clear and flagrant violation of the Constitution to secretly fund a war this way," says Ratner. "And in this case, it was even more egregious because there was an amendment called the Boland Amendment that was passed by Congress. It specifically forbade moneys from going to the Contras. Yet the entire Oliver North scheme was in fact conceived to subvert that Congressional ban on funding the Contras."

"Here you have a member of Congress urging members of the Executive Branch to subvert a law passed by his own branch of the United States system. These people are officials of the United States," declared Ratner. "One of them works for the Executive, Oliver North, and Hyde is a Congressman. They're advocating going to foreign countries and private sources, saying, subvert our Constitution, subvert the Boland Amendment, subvert the entire structure of the United States Government and our entire democracy and let's just go and carry out a war illegally. Contrary to the law of the United States, contrary to the Constitution, contrary to the separation of powers, contrary to the entire basis on which the United States calls itself a republic."

The overwhelming majority of the largely bipartisan Iran-Contra report committee expressed deep concerns about the attitudes expressed by the Reagan Administration regarding the secret funding of a war. "Suffice to say," stated the 1987 report, "[in the] view of North and Poindexter, a President, whose appropriation requests are rejected by Congress, could raise money from private sources or third countries for armies, military actions, arms systems, and even domestic programs... That is the path to dictatorship...These claims...strike at the very heart of the system of checks and balances. To permit the President and his aides to carry out covert actions by using funds obtained from outside Congress undermines the framers' belief that 'The purse and sword must never be in the same hands.'"

But this never bothered Hyde. "We may well wonder whether our form of democracy is equipped to survive in a dangerous world when we cannot keep a secret," he stated, "and other countries whose trust we need become increasingly loath to cooperate."

Henry Hyde: "Bomb Thrower" for the Contras

Before he became one of Oliver North's most strident public defenders, Judiciary Chairman Henry Hyde demonstrated he was a man who would not hesitate to praise lawlessness and subvert the will of Congress.

According to an entry in Oliver North's notebook on March 4, 1985, former NSC director Robert McFarlane briefed four Republican Congressmen about covert efforts to raise funds for the Contras. Henry Hyde was one of them. Another was Florida Congressman Bill McCollum who, as a House manager, would later join Hyde in prosecuting Clinton for allegedly violating the law.

During the impeachment proceedings, Hyde appeared particularly upset over the possibility that President Clinton had suborned perjury by advocating others lie under oath. But during the Contra war, Hyde himself apparently never hesitated to advocate that others should engage in criminal activity, according to one of Reagan's high-level renegades. In his autobiography, McFarlane noted that "many of the Congressmen, Republicans especially, actually applauded the activities I described. Henry Hyde, for instance, a Republican from Illinois, was a genuine bomb-thrower in private; he went so far as to say that the U.S. ought to find a private way to fund Cardinal Obando y Bravo, the head of the Roman Catholic Church in Nicaragua and a fervent anti-Sandinista."

While there is no documentary evidence that Hyde played a direct role in the link between the U.S. and the Cardinal, it is clear that money flowed from the U.S. and the Oliver North network to anti-Sandinista forces in the Catholic Church in precisely the way Henry Hyde had suggested to McFarlane. Though Obando denied any link to the CIA, the August 31, 1984 edition of the *National Catholic Reporter* reported that "four of the Archbishop's principal financial supporters...have been repeatedly linked with CIA operations and anti-Communist church organizations in Latin America.

"The Reagan Administration funneled CIA money to virtually every segment of the internal opposition, from the Roman Catholic Church, to the newspaper *La Prensa*, to business and labor groups, to political parties," says veteran reporter, Robert Parry, who covered the story for AP and *Newsweek*. One U.S. government official stated, "We've always had the internal opposition on the CIA payroll." According to Parry's book, *Fooling America: How Washington Insiders Twist the Truth and Manufacture Conventional Wisdom,* the CIA's support for Obando y Bravo and the Roman Catholic Church "was funneled through a maze of cut-outs in Europe, so even

Obando would not know precisely where the money had originated." Parry was told by one source that "the Cardinal had expressed the fear that his past receipt of CIA funding would be revealed." The Iran-Contra investigation revealed that thousands of dollars were channeled to a "humanitarian organization" in Nicaragua that Parry later identified as the Roman Catholic Church.

Hyde's suggestion to funnel money to the Nicaraguan opposition through the Catholic Church echoed the Reagan Administration's intention to destabilize the Sandinista government by exacerbating religious tensions in the country. The Administration, along with Hyde and the Congressional Contra supporters, found loyal allies in Nicaragua's predominantly conservative Catholic hierarchy, and in other conservative religious groups both in Nicaragua and the United States. Some of the worst terrorism perpetrated by the Contras was, in fact, carried out in the name of God and religious freedom.

Once the Contra war began in 1981, "Obando, speaking in the name of the bishops, repeatedly criticized alleged Sandinista human rights abuses while studiously ignoring the well-documented and much more deplorable behavior of the Contras. By the mid-1980s, Obando had even succeeded in pressuring many Nicaraguan priests into refusing to say funeral masses for dead soldiers."

In early 1980, a group of advisers to then presidential candidate Reagan met in Santa Fe, New Mexico, to formulate his Latin American policy. The advisers were deeply troubled over the continuing growth of liberation theology and social activism in the Church, both at home and in Latin America. The Santa Fe document, edited by soon-to-be U.S. ambassador to Costa Rica,

Lewis Tambs, states that "U.S. foreign policy must begin to counter (not react against) liberation theology as it is utilized in Latin America." Social activism was the result of the "manipulation of the information media through Church-affiliated groups and other so-called human rights lobbies." Such manipulation "has played an increasing role in overthrowing authoritarian, but pro-U.S., governments and replacing them with anti-U.S., Communist or pro-Communist dictatorships of a totalitarian character."

To support this end, the CIA produced its notorious assassination manual for the Contras entitled, "Psychological Operations in Guerrilla Warfare," a sophisticated tract on the latest techniques of psychological warfare. The manual instructed the Contras to accentuate religious tension by emphasizing popular slogans such as "God, Homeland and Democracy," saying "With God and Patriotism, we will overcome Communism" and "Because we love Christ, we love his bishops and pastors."

Contra radio stations, funded with U.S. dollars, operated from both Costa Rica and Honduras. They praised Obando as the "Cardinal of Peace" and broadcast his Sunday homilies. The Nicaraguan Democratic Forces (FDN) posters proclaimed: "God is on our side" and "The Pope is with us."

In early 1982, Obando was awarded the Institute on Religion and Democracy's (IRD) first Religious Freedom Award. According to Martin Lee, author of *The Beast Reawakens*, the IRD "was established in 1981 with funding from right-wing institutions, including the Smith Richardson and Sarah Scaife Foundations," both of which "have served as CIA financial conduits." Support for Obando along the lines Hyde advocated became instrumental in justifying the war. Obando became a frequent visitor to the U.S., telling the public stories of religious persecution in Nicaragua. As Conor Cruise O'Brien, an essayist who has written widely on religious issues, notes, Obando's "complaints helped the President with the demonization of Nicaragua. The President, in claiming that the Church was persecuted in Nicaragua, could cinch that claim by quoting the Archbishop."

Hyde and the Freedom Fighters

But doesn't Hyde have a point here? What the Reagan Administration did may have been against the law. Yet what was at stake was the freedom of Nicaragua from a communist regime, and our own national interests. Surely that justifies an end run around Congress. Argued Hyde, "I am told [the Sandinistas] will have a 10,000-foot runway capable of accommodating any Soviet aircraft in their inventory...The Corinto Port facility in Nicaragua...is being made into a deepwater port, and I presume the dredging that is going on down there is for submarines...I am told half our imports, half of our exports, three-quarters of our petroleum imports pass through the maritime lanes of the Gulf of Mexico and the Caribbean...So if you flank that important waterway with Cuba on one side and a Soviet base in Nicaragua on the other side, you have a pretty tough situation for the import and export [into the U.S.] of material, troops, everything."

Furthermore, how could abandoning freedom fighters ever be justified?

As Hyde lamented, "These hearings will not explore what our inconstant policies mean to the Contra campesino in the mountains wondering whether he will have any food or ammunition next week, nor the consequences of our unpredictability on our allies. Unfortunately, we will not examine the plight of a President who correctly perceives the threat to democracy and our own national security by Soviet domination of the land bridge between North and South America and who confronts a recalcitrant Congress, a Congress [with] schizophrenic notions of fighting communism..."

But just who are these freedom fighters, as Hyde and others called them? And exactly how were Hyde's champions doing in Nicaragua? In March 1985, the respected human rights group, Americas Watch, released a scathing report documenting systematic terrorist attacks by the Contras. By 1984, it said, more than 3,000 children and adolescents had been killed or wounded by the Contras. Scores of doctors, nurses, health professionals, and teachers had also been killed or kidnapped by the forces Hyde heralded. Schools, hospitals, health centers, churches, and farms had become regular targets for their terrorist attacks. According to Americas Watch, "Contra forces...have attacked civilians indiscriminately; they have tortured and mutilated prisoners;...they have taken hostages; and they have committed outrages against personal dignity." In a report later the same year, Americas Watch stated that, "the Contras, particularly the largest of the Contra forces, the FDN, practiced terror as a deliberate policy."

Reed Brody, former New York State Assistant Attorney General, reported in 1985 in *Contra Terror in Nicaragua* that "Contra activities often include[d] attacks on purely civilian targets resulting in the killing of unarmed men, women, children and the elderly;

premeditated acts of brutality including rape, beatings, mutilation and torture; individual and mass kidnapping of civilians, particularly in the Northern Atlantic Coast region, for the purpose of forced recruitment into the Contra…intimidation of civilians who participate or cooperate in government or community programs such as distribution of subsidized food products, rural cooperatives, education and the local self-defense militias; and kidnapping, intimidation, and even murder of religious leaders who support the government, including priests and clergy-trained lay pastors."

Brody documented one of the more horrific attacks carried out by Hyde's "freedom fighters" that took place at a state coffee farm known as "La Sorpresa," north of Jinotega, Nicaragua. After Contras overran the farm, they killed at least seventeen civilians and kidnapped many others. Among the dead was Jamilet Sevilla, a pregnant seventeen-year-old mother. Brody reported that another young woman, "Julia Picado Gonzalez was in her house with six of her eight children when the attacks started. She grabbed the milk for her eighteen-month-old baby and fled when the Contras entered yelling, 'If we find the women of the rabid dogs in their houses, we'll cut their throats with the whole family…When the Contras overran the farm, they finished off the wounded and dying with bayonets, rifle shots and grenades. Jamilet Sevilla was later found with a bayonet blow in her pregnant belly…"

Digna Barreda de Ubeda, a mother of two, was kidnapped and mass-raped by the Contras in May 1983, according to an affidavit taken by Brody. "Five of them raped me at about five in the evening…they gang-raped me every day. When my vagina couldn't take it any more, they raped me through my rectum. I calculate that in five days they raped me sixty times." According to Brody, "She also watched Contra forces beat her husband and gouge out the eyes of another civilian before killing him."

Mirna Cunningham, a Miskito Indian doctor who later became the Government's Minister for the Northern Atlantic Coast, told Brody how she and her nurse were treated after being abducted by the Contras in December 1981. "While they were raping us, they were chanting slogans like "Christ yesterday, Christ today, Christ tomorrow…And, although we would cry or shout, they would hit us, and put a knife or a gun to our head. This went on for almost two hours."

Brody also documented the case of Maria Julia Ortiz, who had taken cover under her bed when the Contras attacked her house near El Jicaro in October 1984 and mutilated her husband. "They grabbed my husband and they beat him and broke his neck with a rifle," stated Ortiz. "They took him out of the room by one of the doors and they bashed in his head with a rifle and they took out his eye. Then they threw him on the floor and they tied his hands and cut his throat with a bayonet. He screamed and fought…and said that he didn't do anything wrong, but they wouldn't let him speak and put a green cloth in his mouth."

Martin Piner, a Miskito pastor, was kidnapped by the Contras and taken to Honduras in July 1984 to be tortured. "He grabbed me by the neck and put my head down in the water," stated Piner. "When I couldn't take it anymore, he picked me up and put me back in the water again. It was like that for half an hour. They took me from there and tied me to a pine tree in the camp for three days."

These were the people for whom Hyde was willing to advocate suspending the Constitution to support.

Papering Over a Constitutional Crisis

After the reports detailing these war crimes had surfaced, Hyde proceeded on behalf of terrorists attacking civilians in Nicaragua to commandeer the congressional investigation of the scandal and steer it off a cliff. The *National Law Journal* called Hyde "the minority's most effective partisan weapon." Congress had barely concluded voting to create special Iran-Contra investigating committees when Hyde launched his offensive to protect the White House plotters from the political firestorm. "There always has been a vested interest in the Democratic Party to point out in great detail the shortcomings of the Republican administration, and I don't expect that urge or impulse to diminish during the hearings." Hyde warned the Democrats not to let the investigation "deteriorate into an exercise in political cannibalism."

In 1998 the concern was different. During Clinton's impeachment trial, Hyde wanted full and instant disclosure. But in 1987, he led the charge in Congress to insulate the administration officials well before the national spotlight was thrown on the hearings. Hyde was forceful and effective in his attempts to limit both the length and scope of the hearings. His goal then was to have a "lean, mean, small, very active committee with as few malcontents as possible," in order to limit both the length and scope of the hearings. He succeeded in the crucial step of streamlining the House and Senate committees into one tightly knit joint group. "The fewer people in the loop, the more structural insurance that exists to minimize the opportunity for leaks," he worried. Even then, as the hearings proceeded, Hyde complained that there is a "lot of piling on by committee members who seem anxious to turn the hearings into an inquiry designed to nail somebody to the wall."

But isn't a strong defense of a Republican president by a Republican congressman to be expected? Perhaps. But Hyde occupied the extreme end of a partisan spectrum. Republican Senator Warren Rudman was quite angered by Hyde's comments: "The people who say that, of course, know little about hearings and less about prosecutions." Rudman continued that "if anyone thinks that the oath they took as a member of the United States Congress...gave them some role as defender of anybody other than the truth, [that person] either hasn't read the Constitution or doesn't understand it." Hyde retorted with a thinly veiled swipe at Rudman and Senator William Cohen, saying they were "vying for first place in the vigorous questions department."

Granting Immunity to Circumvent Justice

Perhaps the most effective action to scuttle investigation of the scandal taken by Hyde and other pro-Contra members of the joint committee was to grant North and other key figures immunity. On January 13, 1987, Independent Counsel Lawrence Walsh wrote a thirteen-page legal memorandum urging the House and Senate not to grant immunity until he had completed his inquiry. In it he warned that grants of limited immunity could create "serious and insurmountable barriers to the prosecution of the immunized witnesses."

If immunity were granted, Walsh pointed out, then the independent counsel would only be able to prosecute a witness if evidence implicating this witness in law-breaking came from sources other than said witness's immunized testimony. This would be "very difficult" in court. Secondly, immunity would result in intensive publicity, which would allow defendants to claim that "an unbiased jury cannot be assembled" in any future trial. Also, immunity would create barriers for the independent counsel to acquire "complete and truthful" testimony. Walsh explained that prosecutors offer a defendant immunity only after considering "the relative culpability of all the targets of investigation, and after they get an idea of what kind of testimony a witness will provide. While immunized witnesses tend to give truthful testimony because they can be prosecuted for perjury, their testimony may be of limited use since they may only give evidence that can be independently confirmed."

Indeed, the immunity grants from Hyde and others in Congress decimated Walsh's prosecution of the Contragate crew. In a 1999 radio interview, Walsh stated that "the most destructive impact on our conspiracy was the granting of immunity to North and Poindexter by Congress...Once they gave them immunity, we were stymied because the only way for us to get through to the President would be through Poindexter. By convicting him and confronting him with a sentence, it would make him think twice about going to jail in order to protect his former boss. We did convict him, he was convicted of five felonies, but the Court of Appeals reversed it because he received immunity from Congress."

Man of Zeal

Roses for Betsy and Ollie

On July 14, 1987, several days into his testimony before the Iran-Contra committee, it was clear that Oliver North was calling the shots. Most members of the committee were at least sympathetic. Many were overflowing with praise for his courageous, if misguided, secret mission to protect the U.S. from a land-based invasion by the "Sandinista Communists."

Syndicated Columnist Mary McGrory caught Hyde before the cameras at the height of rapture for North's stunning success. "Last Friday, on the fourth day of the reign of King Oliver North, Rep. Henry J. Hyde (R-Ill.) a large, pear-shaped, white-topped figure, was wandering around the halls outside the Senate Caucus Room holding a vase of red roses and looking for cameras to tell the wondrous story of how they had been delivered to his office for transmission to the idol's wife. Hyde was honored to turn delivery boy."

While other Republicans "whined" about the unfair grilling of such a patriot by Democratic counsel, Hyde was already working at a more nuanced level. The Chairman knew how North's appearance would play on the six o'clock news and he was ecstatic.

According to McGrory, "Hyde gleefully disengaged himself from the laments" of his fellow Republicans and congratulated the Democrats on their performance. "I think that the counsels are doing a superb job," said Hyde. "What he meant, of course," stated McGrory, "was that only a fool would want to grill the country's new television sensation. On the witness table before North was a pile of adulatory telegrams as high as the stack of documents he shredded when he found out last

135

November that being a martyr for Reagan could lead to becoming a convict."

Hyde declared at the time that North's widely televised testimony was the most stirring patriotic display "since the first time I saw Jimmy Cagney singing 'Yankee Doodle Dandy.'"

Hyde stuck with North to the end. He was in the courthouse in May of 1989 to celebrate when the jury announced a rather favorable verdict for North, convicting him on only three of the lesser counts with which he had been charged. North was found guilty of aiding and abetting the preparation of a false chronology for the Congressional testimony of William Casey and John Poindexter; guilty of destroying NSC documents; and guilty of accepting an illegal gratuity. But as Lawrence Walsh glumly noted, "The jury had acquitted North of all the charges related to his own misstatements to the Congressional committees and to Meese. It had also brushed aside his pocketing of Contra traveler's checks and the complex charge of conspiring…to collect funds for the Contras through a tax-exempt foundation."

"Hyde was seated next to me in the front row and jumped up to shake North's hand," says St. John's University law professor John Q. Barrett, then an assistant independent counsel. "It seemed a little out of place for a member of Congress to be there congratulating a defendant," Barrett told The Los Angeles Times. Oliver North's version of the story goes like this: "Henry Hyde gave me a bear hug, and turned to reassure Betsy." According to Walsh, Hyde also admitted to feelings of "sorrow," saying, "I'm not sure Oliver North got a fair trial."

Anatomy of Principles: Monicagate vs. Iran-Contra

> *"That none of us is above the law is a bedrock principle of democracy...To erode that bedrock is to subscribe to a divine right of kings' theory of governance in which those who govern are absolved from adhering to the basic moral standards to which the governed are accountable."*

—Henry Hyde, 1999

> *"We were regularly reminded of some bedrock propositions, including the President's duty under the Constitution to see that the laws are faithfully executed, that we are a government of laws and not of men...and that the end cannot justify the means. These propositions, while true enough, deserve a less facile application to the complex events involved in the [Iran-Contra] hearings."*

—Henry Hyde, 1987

Stephen Saltzburg teaches trial advocacy, litigation and professional responsibility at George Washington University Law School and was associate independent counsel to the Iran-Contra investigation. "We saw secret policy being made in ways that Americans don't like," stated Saltzburg in a recent radio interview, "...with lies being told all over the place. The best face you can put on it [was that] it was an effort to bring the hostages home and do it as quickly as possible. But," warns Saltzburg, "when you're playing games with getting money from some countries and funneling it into an 'enemy state,' [it] has the risk of WWIII all over it...to compare Whitewater...to Iran-Contra is like comparing the nuclear bomb to somebody carrying a pocket knife."

"What we were dealing with in Iran-Contra was not just some discreet crime about trying to cover-up a sexual indiscretion," says Robert Parry. "What we had was a serious criminal operation with widespread human rights violations that were occurring in Central America. The Contras were going into Nicaragua," says Parry, "and shooting up villages and wiping out peasants on their way to pick coffee. It was a real bloodbath, one of the most shameful activities that the United States government has been involved in...And they were being sponsored and protected and lied about and defended by the Reagan Administration."

Parry says Hyde played a "crucial role by providing cover..." for North and other White House officials. "It's important to recall that Hyde was not just any member of that committee," says Parry. "He was the key House Republican in charge of the thing and was able to direct and even control a lot of the areas they looked into or chose not to investigate." Reflecting on Hyde's stance during Clinton's impeachment, the journalist and author says he found it "amazing to hear all this weeping and lamentation from Hyde about how sacred the truth is when he was the prime defender of a man who was not only convicted of lying and making false statements to Congress, but was proud of it. North went to Congress and lied directly to the committees...But that's OK, in this case, because I guess he was doing God's work. It's interesting how lies can be useful in some cases and horrible in others."

Former Senators William Cohen and George Mitchell, in their book, *Men of Zeal: A Candid Story of the Iran-Contra Affair*, report that they were surprised that Hyde was willing to base his judgments about Boland on the sole findings of Sciaroni. Their description of Hyde is all the more powerful because it is bipartisan: Cohen was a Republican while Mitchell was a Democrat, both from Maine. They note that "in spite of all the embarrassing revelations concerning the preparation of the memorandum, several House members, including Henry Hyde, continued to wave the document in the air as evidence that the Boland Amendments were ambiguous in wording and uncertain in reach. But most Committee members publicly questioned the justification of the NSC's operational role in aiding the Contras on the basis of such a cursory investigation and analysis."

Cohen and Mitchell noted Hyde's considerable rhetorical skill in undermining the proceedings. Hyde, they noted, "enjoys quoting from conservative texts as if from Scripture...Hyde has a doctrinaire conservatism that is softened by his self-deprecating humor, making him a formidable and effective debater. And it was clear from his opening statement that he intended to debate rather than investigate."

As the *New Republic* observed at the time, the Iran-Contra hearings provided for Hyde the vehicle to not only shine as the patriotic defender of freedom and democracy in the face of the communist menace, but in so doing to deflect critical attention from probing the darkest aspects of U.S. foreign policy. "[Hyde] did not bother with questions," noted the magazine in September 1987. "He did not even pretend to be much interested in finding the truth. He was on the side of the president, loyalty, motherhood, the Marines, tomorrow, the Contras, the American people, the past, the

Founding Fathers, the flag, the sun, the moon, the stars at night, and Henry Hyde. He's never hidden his windbag under a bushel…"

At one point, with North on the stand, Hyde rebuked his colleagues in Congress for their alleged hypocrisy and inconsistency regarding the Boland Amendment. As was often the case, his rhetoric led the Iran-Contra Committee into internal squabbles that undermined their investigation. "Now, if we don't like a law, Colonel, and you guys ought to learn this at NSC…," declared Hyde before the cameras, "you just exempt yourself. You see, we exempt ourselves…from the Ethics in Government Act; no special prosecutors are going after us. We have our own committee of our own brethren that'll take care of that. We are exempt from equal opportunity, equal employment opportunity… Now, if we can't ignore the law or exempt ourselves from it, we play games with the process. Do you know how we got our pay raise?…We waited, under the guidance of the stage director over there, the Speaker, until thirty days had elapsed, until it was vested…And we could all tell our constituents, 'I didn't vote for that pay raise.' That's the way we do things. So there's much to be learned from watching us."

Hyde's tactics worked, much to North's delight. As North notes in his 1991 book, *Under Fire: An American Story*, Hyde's provocative statement chiding his colleagues was the beginning of the end of the hearings as a serious investigation. "…The committee began to self-destruct. Brendan [Sullivan, North's attorney] and I sat there in astonishment as the members turned on each other and their lawyers. Instead of focusing their undivided anger at me, they began to debate each other.

During their internal squabble, Brendan leaned over to me and quoted the famous tag line of those Sergeant Preston radio shows we had both listened to as kids: 'Well, King, this case is closed.' Believe me, it's hard not to smile when your lawyer says something like that."

On Thursday, July 9, 1987, North briefly testified to the Joint Iran-Contra Committee in a private session about the covert activities 'the Enterprise' was ready to execute. Senator William Cohen was at this closed-door meeting and noted, "It is easy to understand why he [North] and Admiral Poindexter [Former Reagan National Security Adviser and North's boss at the NSC] might think it a 'neat idea' to use profits generated by the sale of weapons to Iran to help support the Nicaraguan Contras...President Reagan signed a 'finding' authorizing third parties (i.e., commercial cutouts) to be used in selling weapons to Iran...Several Committee members expressed enthusiastic endorsements of the scheme."

Henry Hyde asked: "Why was this different? Why did you have to lie to Congress, why was this different from other covert actions? You know it's very simple when you have a covert action that everybody agrees with...When you get a controversial one, then you have a whole different problem...The end doesn't justify the means...It's a useful ethical statement, I suppose, but I'll tell you, that phrase doesn't seem to me to establish the moral context for every tough decision someone in government has to make..."

Mr. Bumble Goes to Court

In 1990, former National Security Advisor John Poindexter was charged with lying to both the Senate and House Select Committees about his knowledge of a

November 1985 shipment of Hawk missiles to Iran. The evidence was clear that Poindexter lied, but he insisted that the NSC was exempt from the Boland Amendment, and therefore he did not mislead Congress. Testifying in Poindexter's defense was CIA official, Norman H. Gardner, Jr., and Henry Hyde. Both supported Poindexter's contention that he did not mislead Congress, with Hyde stating that he agreed with Poindexter that Boland didn't apply to the NSC.

The Chief prosecutor in the case, Dan K. Webb, asked Hyde if he was aware that Robert MacFarlane believed that the NSC was indeed covered by Boland. Hyde responded by saying he heard MacFarlane offer that view in his testimony to Congress. But, Hyde said, "That was the saddest testimony, it was sycophantic…It was stroking the fur of the House Foreign Affairs Committee Chairman. It wasn't worthy of a fine man like Bud MacFarlane." But Hyde also admitted to Webb that the chief Republican lawyer for the House Committee had submitted a legal opinion to him stating that the NSC was not exempt from the Boland Amendment.

"There were no holes in the [1984–85] Boland Amendment, and there was no exception for the NSC," says Constitutional attorney Michael Ratner. "Its like how many angels are on the head of a pin…It meant what it said and said what it meant. There was not supposed to be any funding of the Contras by the United States."

Ratner says Iran-Contra was an "executive branch" coup. "These guys lost the vote on Boland and they didn't like it. Henry Hyde lost the vote and Reagan lost the vote because people didn't like the fact that there were thousands of people being murdered; that Nicaraguan women, kids, mothers, farm cooperatives were being attacked. They lost the vote, so Reagan and North and the rest of them went around the law to carry out a secret war from the basement of the White House."

Peter Kornbluh agrees. "There were...several versions of the Boland Amendment," says Kornbluh, "but it wasn't very confusing; they simply got more explicit and it was clear that it included NSC. No doubt about it. They knew they were covered by it, that is why they did this surreptitiously."

In Defense of Mass Murderers

Hyde's attacks on Boland were often laced with strong anti-Communist messages that were clearly meant to evoke sympathy for the so-called freedom fighters, or as Reagan dubbed them, "the moral equivalent of the founding fathers." The law, Hyde suggested, was simply not the issue, "...I am convinced the controversy we are about to investigate does not have to do at bottom line with who broke what law...This debate is not essentially about narrow questions of legality. It is about some passionately held beliefs, one of which is the conviction that democracy and freedom will survive and flourish in our hemisphere and how best to achieve this." Hyde's tactic of supporting the Contras who, as mentioned earlier, had killed thousands of civilians, throws an interesting light on what he believes is the best way to spread democracy and freedom.

"We have been supplying the Contras with miserly little bits of weapons and an unlimited quantity of Boland Amendment[s], " intoned Hyde, "...in the hopes they can roll them up and throw them at these

[Sandinista] helicopters maybe." "Yes Boland may be important," Hyde feigned, "but in the hierarchy of values, don't you think betraying campesinos and peasants and little people who trust you, belongs in there somewhere up next to the Boland Amendment at the top of the hierarchy of values...The notion of betraying freedom fighters bothers you, whether they are at the Bay of Pigs or whether we're taking off the roof of the Embassy at Saigon on April 25, 1975, or leaving them to fend for themselves in the mountains of Nicaragua."

The moral is clear: when prosecuting the president, beliefs are irrelevant, and narrow legality will do. But when Hyde wants something, it's about passionately held beliefs, and legality is irrelevant. His contempt for the rule of law is perhaps best exemplified by his celebration of pardons for principal players in the Iran-Contra affair, granted by President Bush.

Pardon Me, But What about the Law

"The matter before you is a question of the willful, premeditated, deliberate corruption of the nation's system of justice through perjury and obstruction It's not even a question of lying about sex. The matter before this body is a question of justice...This case is a test of whether what the founding fathers described as 'sacred honor' still has meaning."

—Henry Hyde, 1998, on Monicagate

"This act of presidential grace...in the moral order of things far outshines political vindictiveness."

—Henry Hyde, 1993, celebrating the Iran-Contra pardons given by George Bush

President Bush's pardon of Caspar Wieinberger and other Iran-Contra defendants undermines the principle that no man is above the law. It demonstrates that powerful people with powerful allies can commit serious crimes in high office—deliberately abusing the public trust—without consequence…The Iran-Contra cover-up, which has continued for more than six years, has now been completed with the pardon of Caspar Weinberger.

—Judge Lawrence Walsh, Iran-Contra
Independent Counsel, December 24, 1992

During an April 1986 closed-door meeting with House Republicans, Henry Hyde broached the subject of pardons for key actors in the Iran-Contra affair with President Ronald Reagan. Even before former National Security Adviser John Poindexter and Oliver North had been brought to trial, Hyde suggested to Reagan that "if nothing more significant develops" about their criminal actions in the Iran-Contra scandal, the President should sign pardons before he headed out of Washington and back to his California ranch at the conclusion of his second term.

According to several press reports, Hyde wanted Reagan to pardon Poindexter and North with great fanfare, as if to commend them for exceptional duty. Hyde, a man who knows a potential photo op when he sees one, suggested that the honors/pardons be conferred at an upcoming ceremony at the Vietnam Veterans Memorial. Hyde's suggestion was reportedly greeted with applause and cheers from the Republican lawmakers present at the meeting with Reagan. "I like the sound of those words,"

Reagan responded and also remarked at the time that "I still think Ollie is a hero."

"Lying poisons justice. If we are to defend justice and the rule of law, lying must have consequences," Hyde stated on December 1, 1998, defending the House Judiciary Committee's impeachment proceedings against President Clinton. That was now. But back in 1987, the very sensitive chairman felt that for those caught red-handed, being publicly chided was punishment enough. "The presidential pardons of...former government officials for alleged offenses arising out of the Iran-Contra debacle is eminently justified," stated Hyde, in a March 1993 edition of the *American Bar Association (ABA) Journal*. "These men have suffered both financially and emotionally and have had their reputations indelibly besmirched...These individuals hardly are going unpunished." And while Hyde today continually justifies the unrelenting fury of the Starr investigation, back in the days of Iran-Contra he saw Judge Walsh, a lifetime Republican, as being overly prosecutorial. "It is impossible," Hyde stated, "to ignore the intimidation factor imposed on a prosecution target by the overwhelming personnel and financial resources of the office of independent counsel, all designed to compel a guilty plea and 'cooperation' or face bankruptcy and possibly jail."

From start to finish, Hyde always treated the Iran-Contra investigation as a partisan attempt to soil the good name of Ronald Reagan. The real culprits, he always asserted, were Congress and the Independent Counsel. "A pardon is not absolution. A pardon is a forgiveness of something that obviously was wrong. But the prosecution was political in nature, an effort to get at Ronald Reagan. So I just wish out of this mess, this six years, and this thirty to forty million dollars that have been spent, maybe Judge Walsh would decide to prosecute a leaky Congress. That would be worthwhile."

In congratulating Bush for the pardons, Hyde actually made the case that lying was justified because everyone has always done it. Hyde wrote, "One would think this is a new phenomenon in Washington, initiated in the barbaric Reagan-Bush administration, hell-bent on 'shredding the Constitution.'" And in an interview on the *McNeil-Lehrer NewsHour*, Hyde again downplayed the importance of telling the truth. "We suddenly get very sensitive about the Iran-Contra situation…I do agree lying to Congress is wrong and it should not be tolerated, but we ought to prosecute it whenever it happens, not just all of a sudden get very self-righteous."

Hyde has warned repeatedly about the dangerous signal that would be sent to future generations if Bill Clinton was not yanked from office for lying about his sexual escapades. But when it came down to Iran-Contra pardons for high-level administration officials who repeatedly lied and took the law into their own hands, the message sent to future Americans was not a problem because the government outlaws meant well. "I don't think that [the wrong] signal has been sent because…after all, their intentions were of the best. I think that's the traditional happy ending, and I'm glad the President had the chutzpah to do it."

Pardon Me While I Pardon Myself

Chutzpah indeed, given that Bush was inside the Iran-Contra loop, and was in essence pardoning himself along with former Defense Secretar, Casper Weinberger, Former NSC Directory, Robert McFarlane. Former Assistant

Secretary of State, Elliott Abrams, and former CIA officials Robert Duane Clarridge, Alan Fiers and Clair George. Bush's pardon of these key high-level Reagan and CIA officials made it possible for Walsh to turn one of them as states evidence to testify against Bush.

Bush explained that he had pardoned Weinberger and the others "whether their actions were right or wrong" because they were motivated by their patriotism, all had "a record of long and distinguished service to this country," and "all had paid a price...grossly disproportionate to any misdeeds or errors of judgment they may have committed."

What Bush failed to explain was that his pardoning of Weingberger prior to trial not only made a mockery of due process and the peoples right to know, but it slapped the final cover on the Iran-Contra investigation, just before the highest Reagan official implicated in the scandal—the former secretary of defense, who had direct knowledge of Bush's own involvement in the cover-up—was about to be tried.

Scoffing at due process, Hyde applauded the pretrial pardons for the Reagan lawbreakers, based solely on patriotic grounds and the good intentions of the lawbreakers. Clearly, when it came to the Chairman's political soulmates, the rulers were appropriately above the rules, and the rule of law and the sanctity of equality was easily sacrificed to the whim of policy.

This stands in stark contrast to Hyde's tone during impeachment hearings when he chided Clinton for being able to allegedly commit perjury and get away with it, while the three women perjurers he dug up and brought before the committee were forced to pay the price for their lawbreaking. When it was a Democrat on the chopping block, the fiercely partisan Hyde was deeply concerned about the message this kind of dual standard would set for our young.

Just as Hyde did throughout the Iran-Contra hearings, Bush went on the offense, reducing the outlandish criminal "Enterprise" of the Reagan Administration to nothing more than a policy dispute. "The prosecutions of the individuals I am pardoning represent what I believe is a profoundly troubling development in the political and legal climate of our country: the criminalization of policy differences."

Of course, Independent Counsel Walsh was not talking about simple policy disputes; he was talking about multiple felonies by high-level government officials, including many counts of perjury, obstruction of justice and blocking an investigation that could have lead to the impeachment of the president of the United States. "Weinberger's early and deliberate decision to conceal and withhold extensive contemporaneous notes of the Iran-Contra matter radically altered the official investigations and possibly forestalled timely impeachment proceedings against President Reagan and other officials," Walsh wrote to Bush on December 24, 1992, the same day the pardons were announced. "Weinberger's notes contain evidence of a conspiracy among the highest-ranking Reagan administration officials to lie to Congress and the American public. Because the notes were withheld from investigators for years, many of the leads were impossible to follow, key witnesses had purportedly forgotten what was said and done, and statutes of limitation had expired."

Then Walsh went on to nail Bush for his direct role in the Iran-Contra cover-up. "Weinberger's concealment of notes is part of a disturbing pattern of deception and obstruction that permeated the highest levels of the Reagan and Bush administrations. This office was informed only within the past two weeks, on December 11, 1992, that President Bush had failed to produce to investigators his own highly relevant contemporaneous notes, despite repeated requests for such documents. The production of these notes is still ongoing and will lead to appropriate action. In light of President Bush's own misconduct, we are gravely concerned about his decision to pardon others who lied to Congress and obstructed official investigations."

"Hyde's Corollary"

It was quite clear that by the time the 1987 Iran-Contra hearings were convened, Hyde understood the full breadth of the crimes that had been committed by the secret White House team. This exchange between Hyde and former Assistant Secretary of State, Elliot Abrams, shows that Hyde knew a good deal about what was happening. "I am trying to change the names you have been called, give you a wider range of characterizations," declared Hyde in 1987. "I know that you are a person who has read some philosophy, and I would like to provide Hyde's Corollary to 'the end doesn't justify the means.' It may if the means are not intrinsically evil, and we will talk about that later...But, as you sit there...an important member of an administration that used a private network of people and logistical support to keep the anti-Communist Nicaraguan resistance alive [for an] administration that dared to use Swiss bank accounts and maybe got taken by profiteers, because United Parcel and Federal Express don't deliver weapons at night in

Nicaragua. And maybe you used some of the Ayatollah's money to help the Contras and went around asking foreign governments to provide funds to keep the anti-Communists in Nicaragua alive and out of the Sandinista gulag. We know those means are wrong and bad and blameworthy, and you have got to sit there and somehow take the flack because you are here now, and you are the only target we have."

Hyde was not merely seeking mercy and forgiveness for those whose crimes he had encouraged, if not directly supported. "These men have all served their country in different and, for some, extraordinarily dangerous circumstances," Hyde concluded in the ABA piece. "For their errors and omissions they have paid a grossly disproportional price. It is fitting that President Bush end his own exemplary service to our country with this act of presidential grace which, in the moral order of things, far outshines political vindictiveness."

Hyde's Heroes:
Pardoning the Rogues Gallery

Just how serious were the crimes pardoned by Bush? It's an extensive list.

Caspar W. Weinberger—Indicted on June 16, 1992, on five counts of obstruction, perjury and false statements in connection with congressional and independent counsel investigations of Iran-Contra. On September 29, the obstruction count was dismissed. On October 30, a second indictment was issued, charging one false statement count. The second indictment was dismissed on December 11, leaving four counts remaining. The maximum penalty for each remaining count is five years in prison and $250,000 in fines.

Duane R. Clarridge—Indicted November 25, 1991, on seven counts of perjury and false statements about a secret shipment of U.S. HAWK missiles to Iran. The maximum penalty for each count is five years in prison and $250,000 in fines.

Clair E. George—Found guilty December 9, 1992, of two felony charges of false statements and perjury before Congress. The maximum penalty for each count is five years in prison and $250,000 in fines. U.S. District Judge Royce Lamberth set sentencing for February 18, 1993.

Elliott Abrams—Pleaded guilty October 7, 1991, to two misdemeanor charges of withholding information from Congress about secret government efforts to support the Nicaraguan Contra rebels during a ban on military aid. U.S. District Judge Aubrey Robinson sentenced Abrams November 15, 1991, to two years probation and 100 hours community service.

Alan D. Fiers, Jr.—Pleaded guilty July 9, 1991, to two misdemeanor counts of withholding information from Congress about the diversion of Iranian arms sales proceeds to the Nicaraguan Contras and other Contra aid. U.S. District Judge Aubrey Robinson sentenced Fiers January 31, 1992, to one year probation and 100 hours community service.

Thomas G. Clines—Found guilty September 18, 1990, of four tax-related felonies. U.S. District Judge Norman Ramsey in Baltimore, Maryland, on December 13, 1990, sentenced Clines to sixteen months in prison and $40,000 in fines. He was ordered to pay the cost of the prosecution. The Fourth U.S. Circuit Court of Appeals in Richmond, Virginia, on February 27, 1992, upheld the convictions. Clines began serving his jail sentence May 25, 1992.

Richard V. Secord—Pleaded guilty November 8, 1989, to one felony count of false statements to Congress. Sentenced by U.S. District Judge Aubrey Robinson on January 24, 1990, to two years probation.

Albert Hakim—Pleaded guilty November 21, 1989, to a misdemeanor of supplementing the salary of Oliver North. Lake Resources Inc., in which Hakim was the principal shareholder, pleaded guilty to a corporate felony of theft of government property in diverting Iranian arms sales proceeds to the Nicaraguan Contras. Hakim was sentenced by U.S. District Judge Gerhard Gesell on February 1, 1990, to two years probation and a $5,000 fine; Lake Resources was ordered dissolved.

Reversed on Appeal

John M. Poindexter—Found guilty April 7, 1990, of five felonies; conspiracy (obstruction of inquiries and proceedings, false statements, falsification, destruction and removal of documents); two counts of obstruction of Congress; and two counts of false statements. U.S. District Judge Harold Greene sentenced Poindexter June 11, 1990, to six months in prison on each count, to be served concurrently. A three-judge appeals panel on November, 15, 1991 reversed the convictions. The Supreme Court on December 7, 1992 declined to review the case.

Dismissals

Oliver L. North—U.S. District Judge Gerhard Gesell dismissed the case September 16, 1991, at the request of Independent Counsel following hearings on whether North's immunized congressional testimony tainted the testimony of trial witnesses. A three-judge appeals panel on July 20, 1990, vacated for further proceedings by the trial court North's three-count conviction for altering and destroying documents, accepting an illegal gratuity, and aiding and abetting in the obstruction of Congress. The appeals panel reversed outright the destruction of documents conviction. The Supreme Court declined review of the case May 28, 1991. North, who was convicted May 4, 1989, had been sentenced July 5, 1989, to a three-year suspended prison term, two years probation, $150,000 in fines, and 1,200 hours of community service.

Joseph F. Fernandez—U.S. District Judge Claude Hilton dismissed the four-count case November 24, 1989, after Attorney General Dick Thornburgh blocked the disclosure of classified information ruled relevant to the defense. The Fourth U.S. Circuit Court of Appeals in Richmond, Virginia, on September 6, 1990, upheld Judge Hilton's rulings under the Classified Information Procedures Act (CIPA). On October 12, 1990, the Attorney General filed a final declaration that he would not disclose the classified information.

Forgiveness Before Punishment?

What are the long-term implications of Bush's actions? What's wrong with forgiving hard-working men acting in the service of their country? Perhaps the best answer is provided by Iran-Contra Independent Counsel, Lawrence Walsh. His description of why Oliver North deserved punishment, which can be extended to other principal actors, is diametrically opposed to Hyde's view. To Walsh, North was a criminal who deserved to serve time for lying and undermining the Constitution. Walsh made this abundantly clear in his "Government's Sentencing Memorandum," of June 19, 1989. "The crimes of which [North] was convicted, involving a cover-up even after those programs became known to the public, were crimes designed to protect himself and his associates, not the national security," stated Walsh. "The fact that North and at least some of his superiors were willing to conceal their work from the American people and Congress and thereby to insulate their actions from the democratic process is, for this defendant, a matter of considerable pride. North has not indicated one iota of remorse for having committed crimes which, because of his position of public trust, jeopardized the constitutional processes of government...

"Certainly, he sees nothing wrong with lying to Congress, when in the view of himself and his superiors lying is necessary...We urge the Court to consider the seriousness of North's abuse of the public trust, the need for deterrence, North's failure to accept personal responsibility for his actions, his lack of remorse and his perjury on the witness stand. Taking all these factors into account, as set forth more fully below, the Government submits that a term of incarceration is appropriate and necessary...Deterrence is particularly important in a case involving not only obstruction, lying and cover-up, but also personal venality...

"A sentence in this case that included no period of incarceration would send exactly the wrong message to government officials and to the public. It would be a statement that fifteen years after Watergate, government officials can participate in brazen cover-up, lie to Congress and collect a substantial gratuity, and still receive only a slap on the wrist. North's view that anything goes in a political controversy would be sustained. Instead, since his acts are a serious breach of the public trust, they warrant serious punishment."

Chapter 5

Henry Hyde on Drugs

In Defense of Treason

"There was no information developed indicating any U.S. government agency or organization condoned drug trafficking by the Contras or anyone else."
—from a memo endorsed by Henry Hyde, 1987

"Fourteen million to finance [Contra arms] came from drugs."
—July 12, 1985 entry in a notebook kept by Oliver North.

The involvement of Nicaraguan Contras and their American support system in drug trafficking to raise funds for war is a matter still hotly debated over a decade after the Iran-Contra scandal came to light. Henry Hyde played a significant role in creating public confusion about Contra trafficking and ultimately steering the Iran-Contra Committees away from a serious investigation of this highly volatile subject that goes right to the heart of U.S. national security. The suppression of the Contra drug investigation was crucial in keeping Ronald Reagan and George Bush from being run out of office for a policy which both fueled America's cocaine pandemic and greatly advanced the mission of narco-terrorists who were busy moonlighting as Contra captains. In deflecting the Contra drug investigation, Hyde also shielded himself and other pro-Contra cheerleaders from the onslaught of bad press which would have inevitably followed public revelations about this very serious issue.

According to the CIA's own documents, Reagan's first attorney general, William French Smith, gave the CIA written permission in 1982 to work with traffickers who were also bringing cocaine into the U.S. without having to report their trafficking activities. By 1985, journalists, law enforcement officials and congressional investigators had a plethora of leads that the Contra operation was riddled with traffickers. "The government made a secret decision to sacrifice a part of the American population for the Contra effort," testified Washington attorney Jack Blum before the Senate Intelligence Committee in 1996. Blum was Special Counsel to Senator John Kerry's Senate Foreign Relations Subcommittee on Terrorism, Narcotics, and International Operations which investigated Contra trafficking in the 1980s even before the Iran-Contra committees commenced their work. Blum told the Intelligence Committee that U.S. officials were "quietly undercutting law enforcement and human-rights agencies that might have caused them difficulty...policy makers absolutely closed their eyes to the criminal behavior of the Contras."

"I put cops in jail for a lot of years for just knowing about a trafficking operation and failing to report it," says former Drug Enforcement Agent, Michael Levine, who served more than two decades in the DEA. "Imagine this, here you have Oliver North, a high-level government official in the National Security Council running a covert action in collaboration with a drug cartel. That's what I call treason," said the seasoned former federal agent. "We'll never know how many kids died because these so-called patriots were so hot to support the Contras that they risked several generations of our young people to do it." Henry Hyde was a "real insider," said Levine, "a member of the House Intelligence Oversight Committee and a good friend to the CIA...Whether Hyde knew about and supported the policy" to work with traffickers "from the start is not clear, but as a key member of the joint committees, he certainly played a major role in keeping the American people blindfolded about the story."

How to Lie on Drugs:
A Hyde Primer

Hyde played a key role in blocking the investigation of the Contra drug connection, not only by consistently refusing to ask hard questions of the Contra plotters, who had substantial knowledge of the trafficking, but by championing a false document that claimed the committee had conducted a wide-ranging investigation into the drug allegations and come up empty.

In a 900-word memorandum of July 23, 1987 to Iran-Contra House Committee Chair Lee Hamilton and Committee Counsel John Nields, which bears Hyde's signature, Robert A. Bermingham, a House Iran-Contra Committee investigator, claimed that an exhaustive investigation by the Iran-Contra Committees turned up no evidence that the Contra leadership was involved with narco-trafficking.

Henry Hyde on Drugs

One got the first impression from reading the memo that all the committees did was to investigate the Contra drug allegations:

> During the course of our investigation, the role of U.S. government officials who supported the Contras and the private resupply effort, as well as the role of private individuals in resupply, were exhaustively examined. Hundreds of persons, including U.S. government employees, Contra leaders, representatives of foreign governments, U.S. and foreign law enforcement officials, military personnel, private pilots and crews involved in actual operations were questioned and their files and records examined…There was no information developed indicating any U.S. government agency or organization condoned drug trafficking by the Contras or anyone else.

While this certainly sounds thorough and impressive, the memo provided virtually no documentation from the hundreds of people who were allegedly interviewed during the investigation. There were no excerpts from the depositions in the memo, no names of the Contra leaders or private pilots and crews supposedly interviewed. Furthermore, there were no quotes from the files, no specific references to which records were examined, nor was there even a reference as to which foreign governments had cooperated in the Hyde-championed Robert Bermingham investigation.

"During the course of our investigation," the fraudulent three-page memo stated, "we examined files of State, DOD, NSC, CIA, DEA, Justice, Customs and FBI, especially those reportedly involving newspaper allegations of Contra drug trafficking. We have discovered that almost all of these allegations originate from persons indicted or convicted of drug smuggling."

Contrary to the memo, all the aforementioned government agencies had information and substantial leads regarding Contra trafficking, at the time of Bermingham's wide-ranging investigation.

Consider what was going on at the NSC and the state department in 1985 and 1986. Oliver North had teamed up with four companies owned and operated by drug traffickers. According to government documents, the companies included SETCO Air, owned and operated at the time by the notorious Honduran drug trafficker, Ramon Matta Ballesteros; DIACSA, the Miami-based headquarters for major traffickers, Floyd Carlton and Alfredo Caballero; Vortex, an air service and supply company that was partly owned by drug trafficker and pilot, Michael Palmer; and Frigorificos de Puntarenas, a firm established by the Medellin Cartel and operated by Cuban-American drug traffickers who also ran the Florida-based sister outfit, Ocean Hunter.

At the strong urging of Oliver North, all four shell companies were put on the U.S. payroll as part of what was then known as the Nicaraguan Humanitarian Assistance Office (NHAO), which was officially run out of the U.S. State Department but closely supervised by North at the NSC. Among those in charge, working simultaneously for the Medellin Cartel, North, the State Department and the CIA, was Francisco Chanes. Also working closely with the network was another longtime CIA contract agent named Felipe Vidal. Vidal had been arrested at least a half-dozen times in the U.S. for drug and weapons violations by the time Bermingham and company prepared their flimsy 1987 memo. Former CIA station chief in Costa Rica, Joe Fernandez, testified before Congress that Vidal had a problem with drugs.

The CIA's Contra-op supervisor, Alan Fiers, and Rob Owen, who worked for the NHAO at the behest of North, were acutely aware in 1986 that the NHAO had hired major traffickers. Among them was Michael Palmer, a former commercial airline pilot, who according to federal court records, "was working for the largest marijuana cartel in the history of the country." When Palmer's DC4 was hit during secret supply drops in Nicaragua, he ended up making an emergency landing off the coast on San Andreas Island, a known haven for cocaine traffickers. Rob Owen wrote to North in 1986 saying, "No doubt you know that the DC4…was used at one time to run drugs and part of the crew had criminal records. Nice group the boys chose."

Not a hint of any of this was mentioned in the memo on the "exhaustive" investigation by Bermingham and signed by Hyde.

In September 1986, Senator John Kerry personally provided the Justice Department with the name of a credible eyewitness who testified to seeing large quantities of cocaine being loaded onto a CIA-connected, Southern Air Transport plane by a man named Wallace "Buzz" Saywer. Saywer would later make history posthumously as the CIA operative shot down with Eugene Hasenfus over Nicaragua in October 1986, tearing the lid off the secret North network. Wanda Palacio, a trusted FBI informant, had provided a detailed statement to Senator Kerry that Pilots for Southern Air were flying cocaine out of Barranquilla, Columbia as part of a Contra "drugs for guns" exchange. Palacio said on two occasions in 1983 and 1985 that she witnessed the operation in the presence of Medellin Cartel king-pin, Jorge Ochoa. But what evidence is there that Palacio was telling the truth about the use of this plane that was also in the hire of the CIA? First, Palacio passed a lie detector test. But even more convincing, Sawyer's flight logs, obtained by Robert Parry at AP, confirm that the CIA/contract employee had flown a Southern Air Transport plane into Barranquilla in October 1985, just as Palacio had claimed.

It appears that in his "investigation," Berminham was interviewing a different set of government officials and Contra leaders than those that had caught the attention in 1985 and 1986 of Senator Kerry and various criminal investigators from a variety of agencies. Jack Blum, while working for Kerry's Senate Subcommittee on Terrorism, Narcotics and International Communications, obtained substantial information as early as 1986 about Contra connections to drugs, which he forwarded to the Justice Department for follow-up. The subcommittee's final Report states that it had "uncovered considerable evidence relating to the Contra network which substantiated many of the initial allegations laid out before the Committee in the spring of 1986. On the basis of this evidence, it is clear that individuals who provided support for the Contras were involved in drug trafficking. It is also clear that the supply network of the Contras was used by drug trafficking organizations, and elements of the Contras themselves knowingly received financial and material assistance from drug traffickers. In each case, one or another agency of the U.S. government had information regarding the involvement either while it was occurring or immediately thereafter."

In stark contrast, the Hyde/Berminham memo of 1987 declares, "Contra leaders have been interviewed and their bank records examined." It continues: "They denied any connection with or knowledge of drug trafficking. Examination of Contra financial records, private enterprise business records, and income tax returns of several individuals failed to find any indication of drug trafficking." Again, no specific mention of which Contra leaders were deposed under oath or exactly what records were evaluated.

But Contra-leader Octaviano Cesar was a direct recipient of aid from notorious cartel trafficker, George Morales, and even testified before Kerry to that fact. Morales, with his own little air force of drug planes and stash of ready cash, was the perfect player in the guns for drugs operation. The payoff for Morales—besides striking a blow against the communists—was a bit of legal help on a few drug busts. "It was a marriage of convenience made in heaven," said a former Kerry investigator, interviewed by one of the authors in the fall of 1986, again a year before Berminham was tasked to concoct his memo exonerating the Contras and the U.S. government from involvement in drug trafficking. The Contra leader, for his part, adopted Hyde's moral stance and roundly blamed Congress for forcing him to team up with a notorious trafficker such as Morales. Cesar said when he dealt with Morales, he "was thinking in terms of the security of my country. It just didn't enter my mind that I would become involved in such a mess…I'm not proud of it, but I just didn't have any choice. I mean, the U.S. Congress didn't give us any choice" but to deal with traffickers.

One didn't even need subpoena power from Congress, to be a DEA agent in El Salvador or a U.S.

Attorney in Miami, to start unraveling the Contra drug connection. Several respected journalists had been following the story since 1984. One of the authors of this book first interviewed George Morales in 1986. Morales, who was also a world-class speedboat racer, was in Miami's Metropolitan Correctional Center at the time. He identified himself as a Contra supporter and a network operative. At the time, Morales was being held without bond on charges that he conspired to smuggle as much as 1,500 kilograms of cocaine into South Florida. In the 1986 interview, Morales said that he was "supplying aircraft and training pilots" for the Contra network as well as flying supplies and materiel to the Contras in Costa Rica. "On some particular days we were loading the planes...and there were U.S. officials around and aware of it and never the planes were touched. Never."

Meanwhile, Morales wasn't the only one doing business with the Contras. Alarm bells were going off all over Florida about illegal Contra activities with drug links. George Kiszynski was a FBI agent with the Miami Office's anti-terrorist squad. According to Congressional testimony, Kiszynski communicated with North through FBI channels. According to a City of Miami Police Intelligence Report dated September 26, 1984, Kiszynski was informed about Contra-related drug activities. A report stamped, "Record furnished to George Kiszynski, FBI," couldn't be clearer. It states that one Contra supporter was "giving financial support to anti-Castro groups and Nicaraguan guerrillas. The money comes from narcotics transactions."

The Miami police document also placed Costa Rica-based, CIA operative, John Hull, and his ranch in southern Costa Rica, on the Contra supply map.

It states that two Cuban-American Contra supporters "are associated with an American who owns a ranch in southern Costa Rica...The owner of the ranch is John Hull and the ranch has an airstrip. In October 1983, a load of ammunition was unloaded on that airstrip..."

Bermingham's brief memo makes no reference whatsoever to Morales, or Wanda Palacio, says nothing about Octaviano Cesar and John Hull or the four drug shell companies hired by the State Department, or the FBI memo, or any of the scores of leads from Congress, law enforcement or dogged journalists. Bermingham does not even attempt to discredit a single source by name. But no matter. He concludes his fraudulent memorandum by stating that "additional investigation of these allegations is unwarranted in view of the negative results to date..."

Using the *Washington Post*

The exact date of the Bermingham memo, July 23, 1987, is crucial, according to Peter Dale Scott and Jonathan Marshall, authors of *Cocaine Politics: Drugs, Armies, and the CIA in Central America*. The memo appeared the day after a story in the *Washington Post* reported that Congressman Charles Rangel's Select Committee on Narcotics conducted a thorough investigation into Contra-related trafficking and found nothing. But the *Post* story was false, so incorrect that it was retracted just days later after written complaints by Rangel and others. In fact, Rangel immediately refuted the claims of the *Post* article, but his response was never printed.

No matter. The memo's use of the false article "helped generate the parallel myth, that an exhaustive Congressional investigation...developed no evidence which would show that the Contra leadership was involved in drug smuggling…The date of that memo is important," write Scott and Marshall, because "it suggests witting exploitation of a lie that had been floated in the July 22 *Washington Post* and that the *Post* itself had retracted on July 24."

Instead of interviewing Rangel directly, Bermingham cited the *Post* story, which was based on leaks from unnamed congressional sources who had been present during a closed door meeting of Rangel's Select Narcotics Committee on July 21, the day before the *Post* story appeared. So important was the *Post* article to supporting the memo's assertion that an in-depth investigation had been conducted, that Berminham cited a quote appearing in it from Rep. Rangel. He is quoted in the *Washington Post*, July 22, 1987, as stating "his investigation," which started in June of 1986 and includes reams of testimony from hundreds of witnesses, "developed no evidence which would show that Contra leadership was involved in drug trafficking."

Again Bermingham is pumping up the illusion that hundreds of witnesses had been interviewed and no credible information exists to implicate the Contra leadership in trafficking, without naming a single witness who was interviewed. In fact, Peter Dale Scott happened to be a witness at the Rangel committee meeting referred to in the *Post* story that was memorialized by Berminham. Scott had been invited to testify at the July 21, 1987 closed-door executive session of the House Select Committee on Narcotics Abuse and Control. According to *Cocaine Politics*, he and a colleague "submitted a written brief on this subject, as did witnesses from two other groups. They gave instances of Contra leaders and supporters who had been indicted and/or convicted on drug charges."

Bermingham could have gone straight to Rangel, but he didn't. It would seem obvious that face-to-face interviews with congressional colleagues would be infinitely more reliable than second-hand news reports that were refuted and swiftly retracted the day after they were published. In fact, Robert Weiner, counsel for Rangel's House Select Committee on Narcotics Abuse and Control, had complained publicly about the incident at the time and was quoted in the *Boston Globe* saying that the Rangel committee, "did indeed find that there is substance to many of the allegations [about Contra drug smuggling]. Mr. Bermingham is wrongly prejudging a congressional committee investigation."

Material submitted to the Rangel committee and boldly referenced in a syndicated *Newsday* article, co-authored by Polk award-winning journalist, Robert Knight, is an eight-page document from the Rangel's Narcotics Committee Counsel, Ronald A. LeGrand, dated June 25, 1986—drafted more than a year before the Bermingham memo. According to the June 1986 memo to the Rangel Committee's Chief of Staff, John T. Cusack, "A number of individuals who supported the Contras and who participated in Contra activity in Texas, Louisiana, California and Florida as well as in Honduras, Nicaragua and Costa Rica, have suggested that cocaine is being smuggled into the United States through the same infrastructure which is procuring, storing and transporting weapons, explosives, ammunition and military equipment for the Contras from the United States."

The 1986 Rangel memo lays out with some specificity key aspects of the Contra drug operation as they would later be confirmed by the CIA's own Inspector General's Report. And it even alludes to the operations of the seafood importing companies later hired by North and the NHAO to assist the Contra resupply operation. "One conspiracy described by these sources involves members of Brigade 2506 in Miami [Cuban-American veterans of the failed Bay of Pigs invasion] and unidentified Colombian drug traffickers smuggling drugs to the United States using two mechanisms.

"The first is to blast-freeze cocaine in seafood at processing plants in Limon, Costa Rica, and then to smuggle the cocaine in through Miami. The second is to use airstrips on the Costa Rican-Nicaraguan border, controlled or managed by American supporters of the Contras, for refueling of drug planes on the way to the United States from Colombia," stated the memo.

The narcotics committee document also refers to the now widely reported 1983 "Frogman Case" in which federal agents seized hundreds of pounds of cocaine and tens of thousands of dollars in drug monies as divers for the traffickers attempted to unload the contraband from a freighter at San Francisco's Pier 96. "Three years after their convictions, two defendants said they had been working for the Contras and had in the past provided Costa Rican-based Contra groups with about $500,000 in funds, the majority of which came from cocaine sales. One of the two, Julio Zavala, obtained the release of the seized $36,020 after producing letters from the Contra-connected Conservative Party of Nicaraguans in Exile and Nicaraguan Democratic Union-Nicaraguan Revolutionary Armed Force."

Also according to the syndicated *Newsday* article, Jonathan Winer, now a high-level narcotics official in the State Department and a former aid to John Kerry, stated in May of 1987 that he was "confident" that drug money was used to help finance the Contras and that North could be involved. "We have received a variety of allegations about drug connections to the Contras and to parts of the North network," said Jonathan Winer, "As to whether Oliver North is involved in that, I cannot say. But members of the North network allegedly were, and that needs to be looked at very seriously."

The article also referenced the fact that former ambassador to El Salvador, Robert White, told the House Subcommittee on Western Hemispheric Affairs in October 1986 that "the Contras have been involved in a wide range of criminal activities that violate U.S. law. These activities include narcotics trafficking, arms smuggling, various currency offenses and other crimes up to and including murder."

As Scott and Marshall report, "Rangel promptly wrote a four-point letter of denial [of the July 22 *Washington Post* story], but the *Post* declined to publish it; the paper merely corrected the false claim about hundreds of witnesses being interviewed." Thus "the 'hundreds of witnesses' and the false quotation from Congressman Rangel were enshrined" in the fraudulent memo about Contra drug trafficking.

In short, the issue of drugs and the Contras had massive evidence indicating further investigation was warranted. But Bermingham makes no specific reference in his memo to having investigated any of the material referenced in the 1986 Rangel memo and syndicated by *Newsday*. Hyde was apparently not interested in any of this either. For his part, he highlighted the fraudulent memo in the minority section of the final Iran-Contra report that was not released until November of 1987— several months after the document had already been shown to be false. Unabashedly repeating the lie, Hyde scolded members of Congress and attacked the largely bi-partisan majority for not giving the false memo more prominence in the final Iran-Contra report, despite the fact that it had been discredited. Hyde stated that Contra drug allegations were created out of whole cloth to damage the esteemed reputation of the Nicaraguan anti-Communist resistance.

"[T]he fact is that the Committees' staff left no stone unturned in its efforts to obtain information that might be politically damaging to the Resistance...," stated Hyde and the others in a footnote to the final Iran-Contra report. "The Committees' investigators reviewed major portions, if not all, of the Contras' financial records; met with witnesses who alleged the Resistance was involved in terrorism or drug-running; investigated the financial conduct of the NHAO program...received no credible evidence of misconduct by the Resistance. It came as little surprise, of course, that the Committees' majority does not explicitly acknowledge this...For this reason, suggestions that the Committees have not investigated such matters, and other Committees of Congress should, ought to be seen for what they are: political harassment by Congressional opponents of the Resistance."

Smoking Guns

While more is now known about the drug traffickers that collaborated with North and the CIA in funding and running the Contra operation, there was more than enough information back in the mid-'80s to give Hyde and other Contra supporters pause.

Among the most troubled and vocal critics of Hyde's actions are members of the law enforcement community. Former DEA cop, Michael Levine, strongly believes North, and those who shielded him such as Hyde, should have been tried for trafficking and treason for their role in the Contra drug operation and the cover-up.

Levine starts to fume when he considers various entries in North's diaries from his heady days as chief gringo Contra commander. He rattles off a cite from North's notebooks: July 12, 1985, "Fourteen million to finance [Contra arms] came from drugs," Levine quotes North. "What the hell does that mean, and where does Congressman Hyde think the drugs went that paid for the Contra's weapons? Into kids' bodies," says Levine.

"If I was working North's case," said the experienced drug warrior, "I would have tracked him and the rest of them, from the time they got up in the morning until the time they went to bed at night."

"There was plenty of hard evidence," says Levine who has written several books on the subject and has testified regularly as a court-certified expert witness in drug-related cases. "The totality of the whole picture is very compelling; this is very damning evidence. We had informants who testified before Kerry, the agents testified. Even in my book, *Big White Lie*, I testified that the CIA stopped us from indicting the Bolivian government at the same time Contra assets were going down there to pick up drugs. When you put it all together you have much more evidence to convict Ollie North, [former high level CIA official] Dewey Claridge and all the way up the line, than they had in any John Gotti case."

"I had my own evidence," said Levine, "a DEA report that states that the CIA stopped us from indicting the same people who were selling the Contras drugs. That's direct evidence, you cannot get better than that. That is a smoking gun. I know this as an investigator [who] put thousands of Americans in jail personally and then indirectly tens of thousands, because of all the investigations I handled as supervisor for seventeen years. I know there was far more evidence already documented, already testified to in secret and open session in Congress. Put it together with Ollie North's notebooks and with his e-mail you have more than enough to put that man away."

Hyde may not have taken Levine's concerns seriously, but the entire Costa Rica Justice Department did, not to mention the Country's former President, Nobel Laureate, Oscar Arias. Oliver North, former Reagan NSC chief, Admiral Poindexter, John Hull, Richard Secord and former Costa Rican CIA Chief of Station, Joe Fernendez, were banned from ever setting foot on Costa Rican soil again, as a result of their Contra activities. Hull, whose ranch was a major transshipment point for Contra drugs and guns, was arrested and indicted in Costa Rica on trafficking charges in 1989. But before he was forced to stand trial, he was secretly flown out of the country on a flight arranged by U.S. officials. Perhaps no one feels the frustration more deeply than Celerino Castillo III. The one-time police officer and Vietnam veteran joined the DEA in 1979. "Cele" Castillo served as a top DEA agent in Central America from 1985 to 1991. Working undercover in El Salvador, Castillo learned about the Contra operation at Ilopango, the El Salvadoran military airport in 1986. "They were running narcotics and weapons out of Ilopango to support the Contras," said Castillo during more than a dozen interviews between 1993 and 1997. "We're talking about very large quantities of cocaine and millions of dollars…There's no doubt about it; we saw the cocaine and the boxes full of money." Castillo said the operation was run out of "hangars four and five controlled by North and the CIA with Felix Rodriguez. The cocaine was trans-shipped from Costa Rica through El Salvador and into the United States…"

The DEA veteran agent detailed how known traffickers with multiple DEA files used Hangars Four and Five in Ilopango for drug smuggling. Despite their backgrounds, stated Castillo, the traffickers had obtained U.S. visas. Castillo said that his reports were very thorough and included "not only the names of traffickers, but their destinations, flight paths, tail numbers and the date and time of each flight."

According to Castillo, the drug planes flown by Contra pilots came from Costa Rica and sometimes the drugs came on military aircraft from Panama. The top drug pilot flying for the Contra network at that time was Francisco Guirola Beeche. Guirola's name was all over DEA databases, according to Castillo, and their aircraft was on a watch list for drug trafficking. Guirola was arrested with nearly six million dollars in drug money by federal agents in Texas, according to Castillo and numerous public reports. Yet Guirola was immediately set free. Authorities kept the money but sent the drug trafficker on his way in his drug plane. Soon after, Guirola joined the Contra operation as a key pilot. According to Castillo there were eleven separate DEA files regarding

Guirola's trafficking, yet he receives no mention in Bermingham's memo.

Felix and Henry

Henry Hyde took particular pride in welcoming Bay of Pigs veteran, Felix Rodriguez to the Iran-Contra hearings. Hyde was proud to stand side-by-side with such a legendary anti-Communist patriot and freedom fighter. Rodriguez was a paramilitary specialist and a CIA agent who was credited with tracking down and executing Cuban revolutionary leader Che Guevara.

With few questions and only praise for his witness, Hyde showed little interest in what Rodriguez might know about the drug-connected operation he was supervising at Illopongo. When it came to Rodriguez, Hyde was ready to justify anything he might do to beat back the Communists and prevent them from attacking over the "land bridges" to North America. "I know there is a zeal among some to confine this inquiry to who did what, and ignore why. And I just want to make the point that I think why some of these things were done contributes to a fuller understanding of who and what [was done], and that the nonfeasance of Congress may well turn out to be every bit as important as the misfeasance or malfeasance of certain individuals."

Rodriguez, a.k.a. Max Gomez, was in charge of the day-to-day operations at Ilopango where the Contra's illegal supply network was based. Rodriguez was placed in the field through George Bush's Office and then CIA Central American task-force chief Allan Fiers. Rodriguez was essentially the CIA cutout, running the day-to-day operations of the Contra resupply network after the CIA involvement was formally forbidden by Boland. It would later be Rodriguez who called Bush's office to alert the Vice-President that Eugene Hasenfus had been shot down over Nicaragua on October 5, 1986. Working alongside Rodriguez as "number two man" at Ilopango, was Luis Posada Carrilles. Posada was credited with the 1976 terrorist attack on a Cubana Airlines jet carrying seventy-three people. The plane exploded soon after takeoff, killing all the passengers, including the entire Cuban national fencing team.

Besides being an anti-Cuban terrorist, Posada had a long history with the Mafia in South Florida. In the early 1970s, the DEA had received documentary evidence that Posada was smuggling narcotics into the U.S. CIA and DEA files are full of references to Posada's connections to major drug traffickers and mobsters. As early as 1974, the DEA was aware that Posada was trading weapons for cocaine. In fact, Posada began working with Rodriguez at Ilopango right after his escape from a Venezuelan prison where he was being held for the attack on the Cuban airliner.

There was not a mention in the false Bermingham memo to Posada's checkered past that had been documented by U.S. government officials starting twenty-five years before the Iran-Contra committees were formed.

Hyde was not interested in pursuing any of the leads with Rodriguez regarding Contra narco-terrorism, despite Rodriguez's obvious links and knowledge. Hyde seemed to be much more interested in what happened at the Bay of Pigs than what a CIA-created terrorist network of traffickers and assassins were doing in the name of U.S. democracy. "Now, Mr. Rodriguez, you participated in the Bay of Pigs fiasco?" "Yes, sir," Rodriguez answered proudly. One of the few truths Rodriguez would tell Congress.

According to subsequent testimony before Congress and later in U.S. federal court at the trial of Manuel Noriega, Rodriguez was also the conduit for a $10 million contribution from the Medellin cartel to the Contras. According to testimony before Senator John Kerry's Subcommittee on Narcotics and International Terrorism, the $10 million in drug money was laundered through Frigorificos. The $10 million in drug money was also confirmed at the Noriega trial by Carlos Lehder, the Medellin cartel's former transportation chief, and Ramon Milian Rodriguez, the former accountant for the Medellin cartel.

Nicaraguan pilot, Marcos Arguado, also worked with Rodriguez at Illopango. Arguado, was the chief pilot for Contra forces in Costa Rica, but after being deported from Costa Rica on drug-trafficking charges, Arguado became a colonel in the Salvadoran Air Force and a key operative in the Contra supply operation. He planned flights from Ilopango that flew to the U.S., according to Cele Castillo.

Songs for Henry

In 1984, Honduran General José Bueso Rosa was indicted for a plot to assassinate President Roberto Suazo Cordova of Honduras and stage a cocaine-funded coup. Bueso Rosa was determined to terminate President Cordova because he had fired Army Chief General Gustavo Alvarez, a key Contra supporter. The coup plotters were arrested in Florida in a FBI sting. The Feds seized over 700 pounds of cocaine during the bust at a tiny, remote airport.

After Bueso Rosa, one of the CIA's key Contra operatives in Honduras, was arrested for plotting the drug-funded assassination of a foreign head of state on U.S. soil, North himself leapt into action, leaving a trail of documentary evidence that any serious joint Senate/House investigation could have tracked. His mission, as he noted in a memo to Admiral Poindexter, was to take measures to assure that Bueso Rosa would not "start singing songs that nobody wants to hear."

"I want to hear those songs," said Levine, "and I think the American people have a right to hear those songs so they don't get ripped-off by government officials who are committing treason, by participating in and turning a blind eye to international drug trafficking in the name of national security." Levine said he is still outraged by North's outspoken defense of Bueso Rosa, "even after he was convicted for the cocaine plot...It was surreal and indefensible."

Despite the fact that Bueso Rosa had participated in five FBI-monitored meetings during which the assassination was discussed, North worked studiously behind the scenes to have Bueso Rosa released and deported without fanfare. North told Justice Department officials repeatedly that Bueso Rosa was essentially misled and didn't know what was going on.

For his part, Henry Hyde never asked North a single question about the sordid Bueso Rosa affair, despite the fact that the story surfaced in the press and bounced around Washington between the Justice Department and Congress and had an extensive paper trail. Again there was no mention of Bueso Rosa in the Bermingham investigation that included hundreds of key Contra supporters and endless documents.

The Seal of Approval

A mountain of evidence now exists to back up the fact that the Contras were connected with major cartel trafficking operations, according to the CIA's own Inspector General. The evidence shows that from its very inception, the CIA knew the Contras were involved in wide-ranging "criminal activities," including terrorist bombings, hijackings and narcotics trafficking to advance the Contra cause. According to the 1998 CIA Inspector General's Report, by 1981 Contra operatives had already brought their first shipments of cocaine into the U.S. for distribution. Even more dramatically, the report confirms that dozens of drug traffickers and trafficking entities associated with the Medellin drug cartel were involved in a secret collaborative effort with U.S. officials to keep the Contras in bread and bullets.

In fact, based on the Inspector General's report, citizens from Oakland and Los Angeles, California filed two federal class action suits on March 15, 1999 against the CIA for protecting Contra traffickers. According to attorneys on the lawsuits, "Each lawsuit concerns two classes of people affected by the crack cocaine epidemic: plaintiffs, largely African American, who experienced harms on an individual basis (babies born addicted; deaths in drive-by shootings); and plaintiffs who experienced injuries suffered by the community as a whole (emergency rooms inundated; business districts gutted). If it had not been for the...policy of deliberate silence, the commencement of the crack cocaine epidemic in South Central Los Angeles during that era could have been avoided or greatly reduced."

Yet, because of the early cover-up by Hyde and other pro-Contra forces in Congress and the executive branch, not only did North, the CIA and other key officials escape serious investigation and prosecution on drug charges, but the former Lieutenant Colonel almost won a Senate seat and more recently was given a talk show on CNBC. Hyde to this day has yet to disavow his relationship with North, despite what is now known.

On March 4, 1991, Henry Hyde was awarded a CIA Seal Medallion by then Director of Central Intelligence, William Webster. Hyde was granted the high honor for his "tremendous service" and "sustained outstanding support" to the CIA. Hyde characterized his own daring-do with the spy agency, as "a rare adventure." Hyde did render a tremendous service to the agency by helping to keep the lid on some of its darkest secrets, including its illicit relationships with drug traffickers and terrorists during the Contra war. Unlike his Iran/Bosnia investigation when Hyde complained bitterly about the Clinton administration's refusal to declassify documents, based on claims of national security, Hyde cherished secrecy during Iran-Contra.

It was executive claims of secrecy and national security that prevented a full airing of Iran-Contra. Such claims ultimately protected the CIA and the Chief Executive for jumping into bed with narcotics traffickers and terrorists. Secrecy and claims of national security, according to former Independent Counsel Walsh, were the CIA's best allies against prosecution.

Walsh made this point in an urgent October 19, 1989 hand-delivered letter to the White House. "Unless different standards for the release of information to the courts are adopted by the intelligence agencies," stated Walsh, "we face the likelihood that former high officials cannot be tried for crimes related to their conduct in public office." Walsh told Bush that as the executive branch continues "to withhold this information we lose a much more important national value—the rule of law. In summary, I believe that concern for the preservation of secrets relating to national security is being used in exaggerated form and will defeat necessary prosecutions of high government officers."

Walsh was right on the money. Despite the CIA's huge role in the illegal war and its direct involvement with drug traffickers throughout the war, not a single officer or high level official served a single day behind bars. Those who were indicted, such as former CIA Deputy Director, Claire E. George, and former CIA Costa Rican Station Chief, Joe Fernandez, either had their cases dismissed for lack of (unclassified) evidence or were simply pardoned.

Post Script

The Iran-Contra committees never asked serious questions or even sought out some of the information that was on the public record, says Robert Parry. The former AP reporter now edits *I.F Magazine* and *The Consortium* on the Internet. Parry wrote the first story with Brian Barger on Contra-related trafficking in 1985. Parry says the fraudulent Bermingham memo that Hyde used had a "significant impact" in the suppression of the Contra-drug investigation. "It was significant because a big part of Iran-Contra should have been an investigation of Contra drug trafficking," said Parry. "There are several points when the investigation could have taken place and a key point was right then when they pushed the fraudulent memo on Hamilton who was so easily dissuaded from doing anything, because he was such a wimp."

Henry Hyde on Drugs

Parry recalled the day two men were dragged out of the Senate hearing room when they stood up during North's testimony and demanded an end to the silence on the Contra drug connections. "They said, 'ask about the cocaine' and they were dragged off," said Parry. "One of the reasons nobody asked about the cocaine was because they had supposedly 'investigated' the cocaine, had hundreds of interviews and found no evidence. Of course, there was no real investigation," said Parry, because anytime investigators from several other committees besides Iran-Contra tried to raise the topic they were "absolutely clobbered and the media was being used to put them down" every time they came near the subject. "*The Washington Times*, the *Washington Post, New York Times*, everybody was being enlisted to kind of beat up on anyone who was looking for the truth." Parry himself took a clobbering, and was pushed out of the mainstream because he refused to back off the story. "We now know," he said, "based on the CIA's report that it was true. The Medallion cartel and the Reagan administration were in it very tight."

Chapter 6

Democracy by Martial Law

A "Prudent Plan"

In over two hundred years of its history, the U.S. Constitution has never been suspended, nor does the cherished document contain any amendment, clause or provision for its suspension. But during Iran-Contra, Oliver North and other Reagan national security extremists were tasked to create a plan to suspend the Constitution and declare martial law—which included measures to detain thousands of "criminal aliens" and "internal" dissenters, and to put military commanders in charge of all state and local governments. "Some of President Reagan's top advisers have operated a virtual parallel government outside the traditional Cabinet departments and agencies almost from the day Reagan took office," stated a riveting July 5, 1987 *Miami Herald* cover story. "[Congressional] investigators believe that the advisers' activities extended well beyond the secret arms sales to Iran and aid to the Contras now under investigation. Lt. Col. Oliver North, for example, helped draw up a controversial plan to suspend the Constitution in the event of a national crisis, such as nuclear war, violent and widespread internal dissent or national opposition to a U.S. military invasion abroad."

Revelations of the martial law plan raised a few eyebrows. But Henry Hyde's were not among them. The man who decried that the Constitution was in grave jeopardy because Clinton lied about sex characterized a blueprint to suspend the Constitution as "prudent planning."

Between 1982 and 1984, Oliver North was the NSC liaison to the Federal Emergency Management Agency or FEMA, and worked closely with then FEMA Chief and trusted Reagan confident, Louis O. Giuffrida. In the early 1970s, as California National Guard Chief under then Governor Reagan, Giuffrida conceived a series of plans for statewide martial law, code named Cable Splicer I, II and III. As commander at the Naval War College, Giuffrida organized "war-games" in preparation for statewide martial law in the event that "militant Negroes" and anti-war activists "challenged the authority of the state." When Giuffrida was appointed by Reagan in 1981 to direct FEMA, he quickly staffed the agency at the highest levels with former associates from the California Specialized Training Institute (CSTI), a counter-terrorism training center he established under Reagan and Edwin Meese in California, and with his friends from the military police. Guiffrida then created a Civil Security Division of FEMA and, using CSTI as a model, established a Civil Training Center in Maryland that by 1984 had already trained 1,000 civil defense police in survival and counter-terrorism techniques. With the full blessings and support of the Reagan administration, North and Giuffrida transformed FEMA from an emergency relief organization into a national security and civilian control agency.

FEMA developed a secret contingency plan that "was written as part of an executive order" that the President would sign "and hold within the NSC until a severe crisis arose." Under the plan, the Constitution would be suspended, martial law imposed, and military commanders would be appointed to run state and local governments. The *Miami Herald* article cited a June 30, 1982 memo by John Brinkerhoff, Giuffrida's Deputy for National Preparedness Programs, which detailed what martial law would entail. The draft executive order apparently contained provisions for "alien control," the "detention of enemy aliens" and the seizure of their property. The "secret government-within-a-government" was made up of "advisers [who] conducted their activities through secret contacts throughout the government with persons who acted at their direction but did not officially report to them." In other words, FEMA had a team of operatives or policy spies in all major U.S. agencies that reported covertly outside their own direct chain of command to FEMA and the NSC. "Much of the time, Cabinet secretaries and their aides were unaware of the advisers' activities. When they periodically detected operations, they complained or tried to derail them… But no one ever questioned the activities in a broad way, possibly out of a belief that the advisers were operating with presidential sanction."

The Secret Plan Revealed

On July 13, Representative Jack Brooks (D-Tex) asked Oliver North: "Colonel North, in your work at the NSC, were you not assigned at one time to work on plans for the continuity of government in the event of a major disaster?" Chairman Daniel Inouye (D-Hawaii) immediately informed Brooks, "I believe the question touches upon a highly sensitive and classified area. So may I request that you not touch upon that, sir?"

Brooks responded: "I was particularly concerned, because I read in Miami papers and several others that there had been a plan developed by that same agency, a contingency plan in the event of an emergency that would suspend the American Constitution, and I was deeply concerned about it and wondered if that was the area which he had worked." Inouye blocked further public questioning by Brooks, insisting that the matter be discussed in closed-door executive session.

After consulting White House Counsel, Senator David Boren (D-Oklahoma) briefly queried North about the *Miami Herald* article. Boren asked North a few puff-ball questions. "Did you participate in or advocate any such plan to suspend the Constitution...?" "Absolutely not," replied North, sitting up straight-backed, poised and serious. "To your knowledge, has the government of the United States adopted any such plan, or does it have in place—in being, any such plan?" Boren asked North. "No sir. None." That was the end of discussion.

At least in public it was. But apparently there was a good deal of discussion behind the scenes. The contingency plans for martial law, and North's key role in creating them, was at the heart of what was terribly wrong and dangerous about Iran-Contra, according to the committee Chief Counsel, Arthur Liman. Liman wrote in a memo to Senators Inouye and Warren Rudman before the hearings began in May 1987, that the plan represents "the part of the story that reveals the whole secret government-within-a-government, operated from the [Executive Office Building] by a Lt. Col., with its own army, air force, diplomatic agents, intelligence operatives and appropriations capacity."

The notion of the secret FEMA/NSC team was even a bit much for Reagan insider and Attorney General, William French Smith, who hit the roof when he learned more about it. He fired off a missive to NSC Director, Robert McFarlane, North's boss at the time, complaining that

"FEMA has promulgated numerous plans and proposals that are in sharp contrast to the concept of utilizing the existing decision-making structure of the executive branch for emergency planning and response. Recent FEMA continuity-of-government plans feature layers of FEMA operational personnel inserted between the president and all other federal civil agencies. Its mobilization-exercise scenarios continue to assign FEMA the responsibility of representing the Department of Justice and other cabinet agencies at meetings with the president and the National Security Council during national security emergencies...I believe that the role assigned to the Federal Emergency Management Agency in the revised Executive Order exceeds its proper function as a coordinating agency for emergency preparedness." Smith said in the letter to McFarlane, "This department and others have repeatedly raised serious policy and legal objections to the creation of an 'emergency czar' role for FEMA."

The *Herald* article put Hyde's hero North right in the center of the action. "The heart of the secret structure from 1983 to 1986 was North's office in the Old Executive Office Building adjacent to the White House, investigators believe. North's influence within the secret structure was so great, the sources said, that he was able to have the orbits of sophisticated surveillance satellites altered to follow Soviet ships around the world, call for the launching of high-flying spy aircraft on secret missions over Cuba and Nicaragua and become involved in sensitive domestic activities."

According to the *Herald*, the North/Giuffrida scenario as "outlined in the Brinkerhoff memo resembled somewhat a paper Giuffrida had written in 1970 at the Army War College in Carlisle, Pennsylvania, in which he advocated martial law in case of a national uprising by black militants. The paper also advocated the roundup and transfer to 'assembly centers or relocation camps' of at least twenty-one million 'American Negroes.'"

And just what is the mechanism for suspending the Constitution? According to Giuffrida, "Martial Rule comes into existence upon a determination (not a declaration) by the senior military commander that the civil government must be replaced because it is no longer functioning anyway…Martial Rule is limited only by the principle of necessary force."

From Cable Splicer to Rex 84

There was, according to former *Washington Post* editor, Ben Bradlee, Jr., another FEMA secret operation involving North called "Rex-84 Bravo," a FEMA national emergency simulation exercise planned for April 5–18, 1984. In a memo to U.S. Attorney General Edwin Meese, Giuffrida described it as "the largest civil mobilization exercise ever undertaken." Reagan authorized Rex-84 Bravo in his National Security Decision Directive 52. The Directive "was predicated on his declaration of a state of national emergency concurrent with a mythical U.S. military invasion (code-named 'Operation Night Train') of an unspecified Central American country, presumably Nicaragua. While the FEMA exercise was in progress the Pentagon staged its first annual military exercise involving U.S. troops in Honduras, blurring for some the distinction between exercise and the real thing," according to Ben Bradlee, Jr. in *Guts and Glory: The Rise and Fall of Oliver North*.

According to Texas Representative Henry Gonzalez(D-Texas), FBI dossiers on American citizens considered to be security threats were forwarded to FEMA. The list, known as the Administration Index (ADEX), is similar to past military intelligence and FBI lists of individuals considered to be "subversive" or who belong to "subversive organizations" such as: financial contributors to such individuals and/or organizations, writers, dissident intellectuals, academics, etc. *The Austin American-Statesman* reported that internal administration documents revealed a power struggle between FBI Director William Webster, and Attorney General Meese and National Security Council Adviser McFarlane over control of an index with 12,000 names. The latter two demanded that FEMA be given the index.

Bradlee writes that the Rex exercise was designed to test FEMA's readiness to assume authority over the Department of Defense, the National Guard in all fifty states, and "a number of state defense forces to be established by state legislatures." The military would then be "deputized," thus making an end run around federal law forbidding military involvement in domestic law enforcement. Rex, which ran concurrently with the first annual U.S. show of force in Honduras in April 1984, was also designed to test FEMA's ability to round up 400,000 undocumented Central American aliens in the United States and its ability to distribute hundreds of tons of small arms to "state defense forces."

Nothing "Bizarre or Strange" about Martial Law?

Professor Diana Reynolds of the Fletcher School of Diplomacy at Boston's Tufts University believes the martial law advocates of the Reagan era left a dangerous legacy. Reynolds indicates that many aspects of the early FEMA/NSC plan as described in the 1987 *Miami Herald* story, were formalized by Reagan starting in 1982, when he secretly signed a series of National Security Decision Directives(NSDD) that made possible "an intensified counterintelligence program at home and the maintenance of law and order in a variety of emergencies, particularly terrorist incidents, civil disturbances and nuclear emergencies." With the North/FEMA plan and the new NSDD authorizations in place, states Reynolds, "The agency would have sidestepped Congress and other federal agencies and put the President and FEMA directly in charge of the U.S. planning for martial rule. Under this state, the executive would take upon itself powers far beyond those necessary to address national emergency contingencies. This would include everything from "seizing the means of production, to conscripting a labor force, to relocating groups of citizens" to permitting "the stationing of the military in cities and towns, closing off the U.S. borders, freezing all imports and exports, allocating all resources on a national security priority, monitoring and censoring the press, and warrantees for searches and seizures."

North used this enormous power to conduct covert actions, collaborate with drug traffickers and terrorists, and in essence engage the vast resources of the federal branch and its mammoth national security apparatus to prosecute a secret illegal war, funded in a variety of highly illegal and treasonous ways. The new secret structure was perfect for Black Budget operations, according to one former Reagan official "who often collaborated on covert assistance" to the Contras. "It was the ultimate plausible deniability," the *Miami Herald* quoted the official.

A section in the article entitled "Orchestrated News Leaks" documented how North applied his powers to win the hearts and minds of Americans by lying to them. "In addition to North's role as Contra commander and fundraiser, North became secret overseer of the State Department's Office of Public Diplomacy, through which the Reagan administration disseminated information that cast Nicaragua as a threat to its neighbors and the United States. An intelligence source familiar with North's relationship with that office said North was directly involved in many of the best publicized news leaks, including the November 4, 1984, Election Day announcement that Soviet-made MIG jet fighters were on their way to Nicaragua...North apparently recommended that the information be leaked to the press on Election Day so it would reach millions of people watching election results. CBS and NBC broadcast the report that night."

In a 1990 article, Reynolds shows exactly how effective North, Giuffrida, and the other potential actors in a coup d'etat were at getting the ball rolling towards U.S. martial law. Reynolds cites a January 1982 joint paper co-authored by FEMA and the Department of Defense entitled, "The Civil/Military Alliance in Emergency Management" which indicates "that FEMA had been given carte blanche emergency powers to acquire resources from federal and state agencies (including National Guard personnel) and the private sector (banking, communications, transportation, etc.) "for use in civil disturbance operations."

But Reynolds notes even this was not enough for Giuffrida's comrade-in-arms, General Frank S. Salcedo, then Chief of FEMA's Civil Security Division. In 1983, Salcedo called for the further expansion of FEMA's powers "in the areas of survivability training, research on imposing martial law, and the potential threat posed by foreign and domestic adversaries. As he saw it, at least 100,000 U.S. citizens, from survivalists to tax protesters, were serious threats to civil security. Salcedo saw FEMA's new frontier in the protection of industrial and government leaders from assassination, and of civil and military installations from sabotage and/or attack, as well as the prevention of dissident groups from gaining access to U.S. opinion or a global audience in times of crisis."

For his part, Henry Hyde did not appear to be phased by the notion of covertly amending the Constitution by executive order. He said it was his "understanding" that the martial law plan was part of a scenario to protect top government officials in case of a national disaster and might contain a provision suspension of the Constitution. But the man who says he cherishes the Constitution and the rule of law so intensely that he was willing to rip a duly elected president from office for lying under oath about a seamy sexual affair, was not concerned about the precedent-setting plan to cripple the Constitution. According to Hyde, North's blueprints for martial law "are highly classified programs in the event of a national disaster." "There is nothing in them bizarre and strange—it is prudent planning for any eventuality. We can't be standing here and not thinking of contingency planning."

Chapter 7

Making an About-Face
From Iran-Contra
to Iran-Bosnia

"Why, of all countries in the world, did we turn a blind eye to a terrorist country?" Hyde proclaimed on the House floor, referring to Iran. "We never knew we had a policy of looking the other way," Hyde said, concerned about "the wisdom, propriety and concern of standing by while the most terrorist country on earth" shipped weapons.

Was this Henry Hyde voicing concern over U.S. policy during the Iran-Contra scandal? No, all that was fine, heroic, pardonable, and not subject to "narrow questions of legality." Hyde's excoriation of U.S. policy toward Iran didn't take root until the Clinton administration, when he decried its policy in 1996.

Apparently for Hyde, it was OK for Reagan's renegades to lie to Congress and to sell advanced weapons directly to Iran because it was in the best interests of U.S. national security. But Hyde's standards changed dramatically in 1994, when it came to a Democrat taking a controversial policy stand. The highly partisan Hyde would have nothing to do with it, and if it was up to him, administration heads were going to roll, even if the policy was simply meant, misguided or not, to stem the ongoing Serb slaughter of Bosnian Muslims.

Hyde had no tolerance for Clinton's decision to turn a blind eye about the arms shipments from Iran and keep it secret from Congress. When the policy was revealed in a *Los Angeles Times* story in April 1996, Hyde became a leading member of the brigade trying to nail Clinton. He was appointed by Newt Gingrich to chair a select House subcommittee given authority to conduct an investigation into the matter. His committee was given a $1 million budget, even though there were at least two other House committees and two Senate committees already investigating Clinton's policy. Hyde said his inquiry would find out what Congress was told about the president's decision on Bosnian arms and what it was entitled to know. He said he planned to question people in Bosnia and at the United Nations as well.

Iran had been shipping arms to the Bosnians via Croatia since 1992. However, in 1994, Croatian President Franjo Tudjman wished to cultivate closer ties to the United States, so he decided to seek the approval of Washington for the ongoing arms shipments. Tudjman asked Peter Galbraith, first U.S. ambassador to the newly independent Croatia, if the U.S. would object to the shipments. Galbraith checked back with Washington and was directed by the Clinton administration to say that he had "no instructions" on the point.

"Given the military urgency of the situation facing the (Croat-Muslim) federation on the ground and the imbalance in favor of Bosnian Serb forces, the administration did not object to possible arms shipments to the Bosnians through Croatia," said Undersecretary of State Peter Tarnoff in testimony before the House

International Relations Committee. "We decided that we would neither approve nor object to such shipments."

U.S. officials said that the U.S. upheld the law because it was not obliged to impede arms shipments under the terms of the U.N. Security Council embargo. Therefore, Tarnoff added, "U.S. representatives were told to respond to further inquiries by the Croatian government by stating they had 'no instructions' on the matter. The United States has no contact with the government of Iran on this matter."

Yet Hyde referred to the U.S. role in this issue as a "serious problem," in a speech to the House on September 26, 1996. He promised to deliver a report that would document "an incredibly ill-advised policy that was conceived and executed in an incredibly inept manner." He goes on to accuse the administration of making his job difficult by "hiding behind the rules of classification. That is, they are insisting that important information is classified and cannot be shared with the American people due to concerns of its compromising national security."

Perhaps Hyde's point is well taken. But in the days of Iran-Contra, secrecy and national security were right up there with God and country as far as Hyde was concerned, and they took precedent over the right to public scrutiny at every turn. "Now we've heard that a free nation cannot operate in a shroud of secrecy," Hyde said sarcastically to North when he was a witness. "That is one of the great testaments that we've learned from these hearings." But he added, continuing to jest, "our Constitution was fashioned in secrecy. It was shrouded in secrecy...So secrecy has its uses. I'm told the Senate met in secret its first ten years."

Taking the opposite position than he did during Iran-Contra, Hyde was righteous about getting his hand on classified material this time around. He asks if "this classification [is] to protect the national security, or is it to avoid embarrassment and avoid admitting mistakes? This administration has made a great hullabaloo about declassifying information," he told Congress.

Testimony by people such as Ambassador Galbraith under questioning by Hyde was straightforward. Galbraith pointed out that less than 50 percent of arms going to Bosnia came from Iran, and "there were certainly other countries who are U.S. allies that were involved in assisting the Bosnians." Hyde asked, "We could have kept Iran out, then, and accepted these weapons from the other countries and thus not provided Iran with a foothold in this volatile country; isn't that so?" Galbraith said that Iran already had the foothold in the country, which had been created by the war itself. "We were not involved in the business of arms to Bosnia," he said.

Prosecuting a Smile

Henry Hyde was so desperate to find some wrongdoing that his committee pursued, among other things, a report that Galbraith had dated an American journalist while in Croatia. The fact that both were single did not seem to phase Hyde. When his investigators attempted to collect depositions from Galbraith's secretary and another staff member detailing the relationship, his efforts could only be thwarted by the objections of a lawyer. His obvious purpose was to find something—anything—to hurt Clinton during an election year.

Finding dirt to embarrass the opposing party during an election year is routine. But like his defense of a man found liable for organizing clinic violence, like his virulent death penalty legislation, discussed in the next chapter, and like his willingness to defend Iran-Contra figures for lying to Congress to an extent that even many Republicans found despicable, Henry Hyde occupies the extreme end of the spectrum.

Just how extreme can be seen in Hyde's committee questioning Galbraith about the "no instructions" message Galbraith was given from the White House. Galbraith said that a White House assistant had called him to convey the message from National Security Adviser Anthony Lake. He volunteered the information that the assistant had mentioned that Lake had stated his "no instruction" message with a smile and a raised eyebrow. Jumping on this profound anecdote, the committee questioned Lake and the assistant about the report of Lake's facial expression. Shockingly, both said they could not remember the smile and raised eyebrow. Setting a new standard for gotcha politics, Hyde and his committee sent Galbraith's testimony to the Justice Department for a criminal investigation.

Chapter 8

Pro-Death All the Way

Shredding the Constitution and Executing the Innocent

Shaka Sankofa, previously Gary Graham, has been on death row in Huntsville, Texas, for all of his adult life. He lost both his mother and father during the years he was in prison. When his stepmother and other family members visit, he sits shackled behind a plexiglass screen and is never allowed to touch them.

Sankofa and his family have gone through the torturous experience of narrowly surviving four execution dates, the most recent one on January 11, 1999. Sankofa was seventeen in 1981 when he was wrongfully convicted for the shooting of a white man in a grocery store parking lot. The evidence of his innocence is strong, but in the United States of America that does not necessarily mean an escape from state-sponsored death.

"In the evidentiary vacuum caused by the inaction of defense counsel, Shaka Sankofa, a seventeen-year-old who was not involved in the killing of Bobby Lambert, was swept into a guilty verdict and sentenced to death for a crime he did not commit," reads his 1998 petition for writ of habeas corpus filed by his attorney, Richard Burr. "Mr. Sankofa's trial made a farce out of the adversary process," says the document, presented to Texas federal district court in December.

Back in 1981, the young Sankofa was tried as an adult in three days. His conviction was based on the testimony of one eyewitness who presented inconsistent testimony and was manipulated by police to identify Sankofa in a photo lineup. Seven other eyewitnesses to the shooting—some of whom have come forward since the original trial—saw that Sankofa was not the perpetrator. Most were known to defense counsel, but they were never called to testify, even though their testimony alone could have exonerated the teenager. But so could numerous other facts never brought to the jury's attention. Jurors were not informed that Sankofa's gun was determined by the police not to be the murder weapon. Sankofa's attorney, Ron Mock—who made it clear he thought Sankofa was guilty—also failed to interview the five alibi witnesses who were with Sankofa at the time of the murder.

Juror Dennis Graham (no relation) indicated that he would not have voted for Sankofa's conviction if he had been presented with the facts during trial. He remembers the incompetency of Sankofa's counsel. "Basically what he did was just repeat almost what the state prosecutor said," says the former juror. "His lawyers did very little." Shaka Sankofa was not allowed to testify. He says that because of this, "we had no choice of [sic] finding him guilty."

What Shaka Sankofa had going against him was a string of violent robberies committed the week following the murder before his capture. He did not deny these accusations, and was sentenced to a long prison term for them. What he also had going against him was the fact

Courtesy of the Graham family. Used by Permission.

Does Hyde have a message for the innocent people on death row? Shaka Sankofa (formerly Gary Graham) at age seventeen, shortly before being sentenced to death for a crime he did not commit, according to his attorneys.

that he was black, a school drop-out, and from a poor and very troubled family.

"I wanted to scream and I wanted to cry and I, I wanted to do a lot of things, you know? And I was told basically to sit down and be quiet and everything was going to be all right," Sankofa said from behind a metal screen on death row years later.

Sankofa spent his years in prison educating himself, and is now highly literate and articulate. He changed his name from Gary Graham as a way of reflecting his African heritage. "There is no verdict that can be rendered by the racist courts of America, there is absolutely no judicial ruling or opinion that can be handed down that can make me guilty of a crime that I did not commit," he wrote facing his last execution date.

Attorney Richard Burr of Houston, Texas, has been fighting to win Sankofa a fair verdict for many years. His fourth federal habeas corpus petition filed in December 1998 won Sankofa a temporary stay of execution in January to allow the court more time to consider his request for an evidentiary hearing. However, the U.S. Court of Appeals for the fifth circuit denied his subsequent appeal in a February 26 decision. The situation for Shaka Sankofa now looks very grave.

The writ of habeas corpus—the right to a review by the federal courts of any state conviction that might be unconstitutional—is so essential to democracy that it has been modeled by countries and constitutions the world over. Daniel Patrick Moynihan stood up on the Senate floor during debate on the bill and said that he would give up his right to vote before he would give up that right.

But three years ago, Henry Hyde played a major role in profoundly undermining this constitutional right. As a result, Sankofa may have the chilling distinction of being among the first group of innocent people to be executed because of the arbitrary technicalities of a frightening piece of legislation: the Anti-Terrorism and Effective Death Penalty Act of April 1996 (AEDPA). This lethal legislation was introduced into the House by Henry Hyde and championed by him until it became law.

"Few mistakes made by government officials can equal the horror of executing an innocent person," says Amnesty International's Piers Bannister. "In the U.S.A. the government has recently increased the danger of lethal error by reducing the legal safeguards against it," he says, referring to the AEDPA. The bill—which Hyde so enthusiastically pushed through—reduces those safeguards dramatically, virtually assuring the execution of innocent people.

Through a series of new restrictions on appeals, the AEDPA limits the circumstances under which federal courts can hear new evidence of innocence. The legislation speeds up executions by imposing strict time limits on death row prisoners' appeals. It also permits only one federal appeal of a state court conviction, even if new evidence is found. If any subsequent appeals are attempted, it demands proof that the evidence could not have been discovered previously, and proof of innocence "by clear and convincing evidence" even before the evidence pointing to innocence has a chance to be heard. "Thousands and thousands of people now have forever lost their right to have a life-tenured judge, a judge that will not stand for election next year, to determine the lawfulness of his or her incarceration," says George Kendall, an attorney with the NAACP Legal Defense Fund who has twenty years of experience working with death penalty cases.

Under one of the many demands of the AEDPA, Sankofa was required to prove that his current evidence of innocence could not have been discovered earlier "through the exercise of due diligence." Since he could not prove this—and Burr says this is very hard, if not impossible, to prove—the federal courts dismissed the case and will likely send Sankofa to his death, regardless of his innocence. "The requirement that a person with evidence of innocence must also show that the constitutional violation in question could not have been previously discovered means that some—perhaps most—

innocent people will not be able to have their claims heard in federal court," says Burr. Many innocence claims could have been discovered earlier if done so by a competent attorney with adequate time and resources for investigation. But many death row prisoners do not even have post-conviction attorneys. And ironically, the very fact that so many prisoners did not have the luxury of a competent trial attorney in the first place is the only reason they ended up on death row.

"The AEDPA allows for death by technicality," says Burr. "People who are innocent are going to be executed, and not even be heard first. You're considered guilty even with proof of innocence."

On January 25, Burr filed a legal brief with the U.S. Court of Appeals addressing the inequities of the application of the AEDPA in his client's case. "In a capital case where the facts presented in a habeas petition raise a nagging and legitimate question about guilt and innocence, and there had never been a hearing of that evidence of innocence in open court before an impartial judge, can we let the barriers of procedural complexity preclude the hearing that elemental justice demands?" says the brief. It points out that "The one who will die if these procedural technicalities result in applying AEDPA to this case is Shaka Sankofa...If he did not kill anyone, should Mr. Sankofa die anyway so that the state can say that it won the battle of procedural niceties...?"

Regardless of such pleas, the federal court's February 26 decision used the AEDPA to deny a request for a hearing based on evidence of innocence. It acknowledged that "Under the law that applied to Mr. Sankofa's petition in 1993, he is entitled to have his ineffective assistance and actual innocence claims considered on the merits. Under the AEDPA, he will not be." The three judges ruling for the court point out that the AEDPA has made it "significantly harder" for prisoners to obtain a hearing on any petitions after their first one. Yet this does not seem to offend the judges' sense of justice. "We have found no support for Graham's argument that denying federal court review of a successive habeas application alleging that constitutional violations resulted in the conviction of an innocent person contravenes due process and constitutes cruel and unusual punishment."

The judges take this even further. They clarify that cruel and inhuman punishment does not violate the Eighth Amendment unless it is "inhuman and barbarous" or "shocks the conscience and sense of justice of the people," citing previous cases. Expressing a blind faith in the integrity of the U.S. Congress, they say that since the rules of the AEDPA are under the authority of Congress "to curb abuses of the writ," they do not see how these rules can "shock the conscience." Judges King, Jolly and DeMoss then go so far as to reject Sankofa's claim that, even assuming that he is innocent, the execution of an innocent person contravenes the Fifth, Eighth, and Fourteenth Amendments. They reject the Supreme Court argument that in a capital case a "truly persuasive" demonstration of actual innocence would make the execution of the person unconstitutional and thereby entitle him or her to habeas corpus relief.

This appalling analysis has taken the AEDPA to its extreme. And it does not seem to "shock the conscience" of Henry Hyde, who bears much responsibility for the death and suffering that will result. He seems to feel that the death of innocent people is a price worth paying. "We have enormous protections, the best by far, but we're never going to have a system that will never execute an innocent person," Hyde said in a 1997 statement—made the year after his legislation had all but destroyed any "enormous protections" that may or may not have existed before the AEDPA.

Hyde has not just been concerned with constraining the writ of habeas corpus in his crusade to expand the use of the death penalty. One of his attempts at enlarging the sphere of death failed, but shows how far he is willing to go in promoting death. In 1993, Hyde cosponsored a proposed bill to reduce funding to states for crime control and improving street safety if they refused to have in place "a law which requires a sentence of death to be imposed when a law enforcement officer is killed in the line of duty." The idea was to force the death penalty into all fifty states.

Frank McNeirney of Catholics Against Capital Punishment (CACP) commented on Hyde's support for this attempt in a response to Ann Scheidler, assistant director of the Pro-Life Action League. She is the wife of Joseph Scheidler, found liable for masterminding violence against abortion clinics who is one of Henry Hyde's "heroes." In a letter, she requested that CACP "not celebrate the anti-death penalty activities of anyone who supports the killing of the unborn." In the organization's 1997 newsletter, McNeirney addressed the other side of the coin by criticizing "anti-abortion politicians who not only tolerate the death penalty, but do all they can to increase the number and frequency of human deaths by execution." The one example he cites in responding to Scheidler is "House Judiciary Chairman Henry Hyde from your state." McNeirney informs her about the bill that, if it had passed, would have forced states without the death penalty to lose funds. "To us, that's pro-death, no matter how you slice it," writes fellow Catholic McNeirney. "It's not merely allowing killing; it's fostering killing."

The Death of Innocents: A New Judicial Wilderness

As the AEDPA legislation that Hyde ushered through swings into gear, the devastating effects are beginning to show themselves across the country. Georgia is an example of a state where habeas corpus review is a particular necessity. In that state, two-thirds of the death sentences handed down by the state courts have been overturned by the federal courts. This means that two-thirds of the individuals sentenced to death in Georgia have been done so erroneously, in violation of the Constitution. Even so, Georgia's Attorney General Michael J. Bowers went on record as stating that no one on death row has been falsely accused. "There is rarely any question about the guilt of these people, virtually none. That is a myth…these guys on death row are the pits," he said. Up against attitudes such as this, the wrongfully convicted in Georgia have been spared only by the intervention of the federal courts looking over the shoulder of an out-of-control state system. But no longer. This is a fact which does not seem to concern Henry Hyde or his fellow politicians who enthusiastically embraced the deadly legislation.

Nationally, almost half of all death row federal habeas corpus challenges have succeeded because of violations by the state courts. Somehow, the AEDPA has gotten away with turning a blind eye to this fact. It returns a dangerous amount of power to the state courts, where prosecutorial misconduct, incompetent lawyering and other gross inequities are rampant.

Just how many innocent people might be on death row? In Hyde's home state of Illinois alone, eleven people sentenced to death have been found innocent and set free since 1977. Most recent among them is Steven Smith, freed on February 24, 1999. Anthony Porter walked out of an Illinois jail on February 5, 1999 after spending sixteen years on death row. The forty-three-year-old African American with an I.Q. of fifty-one came within a breath of being executed for a double murder he did not commit. Porter was freed not by the legal system but simply because a university professor and his journalism students found the real killer. If this group had not happened to look into his case at this particular time, Hyde's state would have killed an innocent man. There is every reason to believe that it already has, even without the AEDPA.

In response to Porter's release, *The Chicago Tribune* wrote, "Something has gone terribly, chillingly wrong here," and asked whether the state of Illinois will address the problem "before an innocent person dies, or after that happens?" The release led to many other outraged calls for a moratorium on death throughout Hyde's home state. But Hyde's was not among the voices raised.

The good news is that a greater number of journalism students and others with a conscience feel compelled to take on the responsibilities shirked by the legal system. But this is no substitute. In the Illinois capital, State Senate President James "Pate" Philip said that he doubted the state would implement the death penalty moratorium, even though so many men have left death row in Illinois. "I haven't had any of my (Senate Republican) members talk to me about a moratorium. Not one," said Philip on the day of Smith's release.

However, an oasis of justice may be springing up in Hyde's very own district, DuPage County. As of this writing in March 1999, an unprecedented trial is undergoing jury selection. Rolando Cruz was freed in 1992 after spending ten years on death row for a crime he didn't commit. Four DuPage County sheriff's officers and three former prosecutors are facing felony obstruction of justice and official misconduct charges in the landmark case. They are being tried for their alleged roles in attempting to frame Cruz by fabricating evidence of Cruz's guilt and concealing evidence that might have exonerated him. Henry Hyde certainly knew about the DuPage County trial and wrongful conviction of Cruz, but that did not steady his hand as he went on to push the AEDPA through.

Justice Moses Harrison II of the Illinois State Supreme Court seems to be out of synch with Hyde when he concludes that the high risk of executing the innocent undermines the entire justice system. "Despite the courts' efforts to fashion a death penalty scheme that is just, fair, and reliable, the system is not working," he stated during a court proceeding. "Innocent people are being sentenced to death…It is no answer to say that we are doing the best we can. If this is the best our state can do, we have no business sending people to their deaths."

Hyde's state has been highlighted in national media like nowhere else, as the discoveries of innocence on death row increase. If change doesn't begin there, it seems likely not to happen anywhere else. "It's going to take some innocent people being killed. It's going to take people bringing caskets into a hearing and saying 'look, if

Pro-Death All the Way

this is the kind of system you want to operate, keep the Hyde terrorism bill the way it is,'" says NAACP attorney George Kendall.

In the country as a whole, seventy-six people sentenced to death have been found to be innocent and released since the death penalty was instated in 1976. One can only speculate how many of these would have been electrocuted, gassed, shot, hanged or injected if Hyde's restrictions to their due process had been in effect earlier. Even before the AEDPA, it was extremely difficult to free an innocent person from death row. "These restrictions virtually guarantee that the number and variety of wrongful murder convictions and death sentences will increase," said an ACLU press release at the time debate on the bill was underway.

For many sentenced to death, time is the only lifeline. According to a 1997 report from the Death Penalty Information Center in Washington, D.C., it takes an average of seven years to discover and prove innocence of those wrongfully convicted on death row. The average time between sentencing and execution is now eight years—just enough to exonerate those innocents lucky enough to have advocates. Even so, Henry Hyde thinks eight years is much too long to wait for an execution. He called this amount of time "ridiculous" in a Congressional debate, complaining that "if you have multiple convictions, it could take even longer...We need to cut the time delay on the appeals dramatically." Now that he has successfully done that, it is estimated that the time between sentencing and execution has been cut to four years, not allowing adequate time for the often long and slow road of uncovering new evidence and filing appeals to prove innocence.

According to the Death Penalty Information Center, many of the seventy-six who have been freed depended on habeas corpus review to discover innocence, usually after many years. Had Hyde's legislation been in effect at the time, they would have been executed. Clarence Brandley, who was released from death row in 1990, is a living testament to this fact. Brandley was convicted of murdering a Conroe, Texas girl in 1981 and spent nine years on death row. It took seven of those years before witnesses who could exonerate him agreed to come forward. Today he is a lay minister. "In my particular case there was a lot of things that came out after the trial and if I didn't have the time, I wouldn't be here today," he says.

The case of Lloyd Schlup also starkly illustrates the point. Schlup, whose conviction and death sentence were upheld by all the state courts in Missouri which reviewed them, was finally given a chance by the United States Supreme Court to prove his innocence and his lawyer's incompetence. He was absolved of all charges and freed. The federal District Court judge who granted him a new hearing said that if the AEDPA had been in effect, Schlup would not have been given his life back.

Similar to the Hyde Amendment, Hyde's death penalty legislation discriminates against the poor, who have already likely suffered from inadequate counsel before even ending up on death row. While the poor are guaranteed some form of counsel during the trial process, no lawyers are provided for post-conviction review. Thus, many will not be able to comply with the "effective death penalty" time limit to file for federal review, as they won't even have attorneys. Beginning in 1995, Congress cut the entire federal subsidy to death penalty resource centers that had provided lawyers for poor death row prisoners. "There are more people without lawyers with death sentences than ever before," says Kendall. "And Hyde agreed to this. He always wanted to speed up the process."

Just as state laws restricting abortion became harsher in the wake of the Hyde Amendment, now state laws restricting death penalty appeals are becoming harsher in the shadow cast by the AEDPA. The United Nations Special Rapporteur on extrajudicial, summary or arbitrary executions, Bacre Waly Ndiaye, reports that "A movement to speed up executions in state law has also been reported. In some states, laws requiring capital defendants to raise all their claims at a single appeal have been enacted," he points out to the Commission on Human Rights in 1998.

Ndiaye also reports to the United Nations that in Texas—the death penalty capitol of the United States—most of the state judges are former prosecutors, creating "a climate far more favorable to the prosecution than to the defense." Most state judges are elected, so their decisions are influenced by a desire to appear "tough on crime" and get votes, often to the detriment of the person deserving a new trial.

Playing Politics with Atrocity: Hyde Uses the Oklahoma Bombing Card

"Hyde was a very central player" in passing the AEDPA legislation, says George Kendall, who testified on the legislation before the House Judiciary Committee and attended many hearings before it was passed. He argues that, since it suspends the writ of habeas corpus, the legislation is plainly unconstitutional. The right to federal review of state convictions is in fact the only right written into the actual body of the Constitution. Through Hyde's efforts to pass legislation undoing our constitution, the head of the Judiciary Committee has contributed to the historic destruction of a fundamental constitutional guarantee. How did he manage to pull this off?

The crafting of AEDPA had been well underway when disaster struck Oklahoma City in 1995, but the worst case of terrorism in U.S. history was a plus for those pushing the bill. The Senate took the House bill and passed its version only two months after the Oklahoma bombing. To work out their differences, both houses of Congress then met in conference committee, which was chaired by Henry Hyde. A new version was put forth just a few days before the anniversary of the bombing on April 19, 1996, and it restored almost all the provisions that had been knocked out of the House version earlier.

Henry Hyde was able to ride the wave of hysteria following the Oklahoma City bombing to push through legislation that had nothing to do with fighting terrorism, but a lot to do with escalating executions. In the aftermath of the bombing, a nation suddenly made aware of its vulnerability wanted something to be done, and the politicians took full advantage. Somehow, people who had not studied the issue felt that the changes in habeas corpus would help execute terrorists faster. Most did not realize that the limits on habeas corpus would not even apply in the case of Oklahoma City, since it was tried at the federal level and therefore did not require review of state courts. No matter. This was a good opportunity for the right wing to transform the "anti-terrorism" bill into an attack on a constitutional right to death penalty appeals. Presidential candidate Bob Dole even went so far as to say that the habeas corpus restrictions were "the heart and soul" of the anti-terrorism legislation.

Hyde and his gang used the families of victims killed in the bombing, still in the throes of grief, as political tools, bringing them to Washington to lobby for the speeding up of the death penalty process. Under the guise of fighting terrorism, politicians took the opportunity for political grandstanding that the emotionally-charged situation afforded them. When some of the stronger anti-terrorism measures were dropped from the bill, Rep. Christopher Cox joined Dole in admitting that "the death penalty is the essence of this bill."

Yet some family members who lost loved ones in the Oklahoma City bombing eventually saw through the gimmickry of the death penalty legislation and had the courage to speak out. One of these, Bud Welch, lost his twenty-three-year-old daughter, Julie, in the disaster. "A few short weeks after, when they were talking about an anti-terrorism bill, I was ready to be involved in anything," said Welch. "I was all for it. That was the mood of the family members at the time." He says that politicians were able to take advantage of the victims' family members and were dishonest in the process. "I didn't know at first that we had executed innocent people and now have seventy-five released people walking around. Like the others, I had no idea." But some months later, everything turned around for the bereaved father. When his niece, who is a criminal defense lawyer, explained to him the true meaning of the "effective death penalty act," he was horrified and took a strong stand against it.

Welch journeyed to Washington and made a point of meeting privately with Henry Hyde in his office, to express his opposition to Hyde's legislation. "He listened, but he didn't hear what I had to say," says Welch about the meeting. "And what Hyde said didn't make any sense to me. He said we needed to do something to speed up the death penalty, we had to set an example. If we don't execute some of these people, crime will continue. But I knew in the case of the bombing, the death penalty had nothing to do with that. I left Hyde's office feeling as though it had been a waste of time." Welch felt he had been dealt a standard, conservative party line. "It was the general response of all of them. They were kind of in locked step. If you're a politician, you try to get all the votes you can and use what sells well. The one that says he's tough on crime gets the votes."

Welch has become an avid campaigner against the death penalty since losing his daughter, who herself was an anti-death penalty activist. "I would like to go back to Henry Hyde and tell him about Robert Miller in my state of Oklahoma. He was in prison for eleven years, eight on death row. He was released in January of 1998 after the courts found he was innocent based on DNA evidence. It took eleven years. If we had done what Henry Hyde wanted us to do, Rob Miller would not have stayed on death row for eight years. We would have fried him before that. Now he's out for one reason only, because he's innocent."

During the period when the bill was under debate in Washington, Welch played a significant role on the opposite side of the fence of most of the Oklahoma City families. At one point, he joined two wrongfully convicted men who had been freed from death row at a March

1996 press conference in Washington, D.C. Opposing views on the bill were presented in two press conferences. On Hyde's side, the wife of a Secret Service agent killed in the Oklahoma blast fought back tears as she pleaded for the legislation that would limit death penalty appeals. On the other, Bud Welch told the crowd that "The last thing she [his daughter Julie] would have wanted would be for Americans to lose their constitutional rights because of her death." The two wrongfully convicted men told reporters that it was the habeas corpus appeals that saved their lives. One of them, former prizefighter Rubin "Hurricane" Carter, said that he was at the peak of his professional boxing career in 1967, about to compete for the Middleweight crown, when he was convicted of a triple murder that he did not commit. Years later, during his habeas corpus review, the federal court overruled the state conviction saying it was based on "concealment of evidence, rather than disclosure." Hyde's legislation would have prevented this appeal that freed him from nineteen years in prison. "All too often we forget that human lives...are literally at stake. This writ of habeas corpus is not just a piece of paper," Carter said, holding up the court document before the crowd at the press conference.

Since Hyde was across town, it seems he didn't pay much attention to the testimony of Carter. A month later, he told the Congress that "the absurdity, the obscenity of seventeen years from the time a person has been sentenced till that sentence is carried out through endless appeals...makes a mockery of the law."

In this analysis, Hyde did not comment on whether the incarceration of an innocent man for nineteen years makes a mockery of the law, or whether seventeen years was an "obscene" amount of time to keep Rubin Carter out of the death chamber.

On March 14, 1996, a letter from Bud Welch to Rep. Helen Chenoweth of Idaho and Rep. Melvin Watt of North Carolina was introduced into the Congressional record. Both representatives were working hard to strike the restrictive habeas corpus package from the Anti-Terrorism bill. "We understand that while habeas corpus may not be a household word, in Oklahoma or anywhere else in America, it is something for which our founders fought to enshrine in the Constitution…we do not need this legislation to terrorize us still further by taking from us our constitutional freedoms," wrote Welch. "It utterly galls us as a family so devoted to my daughter that we and our loss are being used as a political football for politicians eager to posture themselves as 'tough' on crime."

In a debate with Henry Hyde in Congress when she read Welch's letter into the record, Chenoweth pointed out the constitutional violations inherent in the time limits set by Hyde for federal appeals. She quotes Article 1, Section 9 of the Constitution, which guarantees, "The privilege of the writ of habeas corpus shall not be suspended, unless when in the cases of rebellion or invasion, the public safety may require it." This threat to the Constitution—and the lives of innocent Americans—did not seem to move the Chairman of the Judiciary Committee, even though he has pledged allegiance to the Constitution on numerous occasions.

"We have been moving toward reforming, not extirpating, not deforming, reforming habeas corpus, so justice, justice, justice, might be done, not only to the convicted accused, who has gone up the State system, up the

Pro-Death All the Way

Federal system, and back again, but to the families of the victims," Hyde professed to the Congress. He went on to express his outrage that John Wayne Gacy—the famous, serial killer of young boys—took fourteen years to be executed—as if he is an example of a typical death row case and therefore justifies Hyde's actions. "Members must be sick of hearing his name. I see his face, because I represented where he lived and where they found twenty-seven bodies buried in his house," complained Hyde.

In another debate, Rep. Conyers of Michigan asked Hyde how habeas corpus reform would "deter a single terrorist act." Hyde responded that "the gentleman knows that sure punishment and swift punishment is a deterrence, and that is the answer to the gentleman's question." Hyde obviously had not done his homework on this point. The FBI Uniform Crime Reports show that there has been no change in the national murder rate since the death penalty was reinstated. According to the Death Penalty Information Center in Washington, D.C., the majority of death penalty states show murder rates higher than non-death penalty states. And, experts from the American Society of Criminology, the Academy of Criminal Justice Sciences, and the Law and Society Association confirmed the fact that the death penalty is not a deterrent.

Hyde was indignant about the fact that the amendment introduced by Conyers attempting to eliminate the habeas corpus "reform" did not impose the death penalty for terrorist acts, but joined with all other Western democracies to call for life in prison instead of death. "Oh, the gentleman from Michigan provides a life sentence, but not the death penalty," exclaimed Hyde. "Now, somebody who kills somebody using biological

217

toxin certainly qualifies for the death penalty in my book."

In a chilling statement before the Congress, Hyde explained his motives for pushing for swifter executions. "Now, we have to have some answer not to the use of habeas corpus but to the abuse of habeas corpus. All we are asking, we are not bloodthirsty. We simply say look, if you have been convicted, if you have had your direct appeal, then you have had your habeas appeal through the state courts, through the federal court, let us come to closure and let justice be done."

One month before passage of the bill, twenty-five leading public policy organizations—including the American Jewish Congress, the NAACP Legal Defense and Education Fund, the National Association of Criminal Defense Lawyers and the National Black Police Association—signed a letter to those Members stating their emphatic opposition to Hyde's pet legislation. "The habeas corpus title in these bills would turn back the clock of history, reviving the very injustices we have tried so hard, and so long, to overcome," the letter stated. Their words went unheeded. Believing the next elections to be more important than his reservations about the bill, President Clinton signed it into law on April 24, 1996.

The Sweet Smell of Success

The legislation has already killed at least one man who was a victim of illegal conduct by a prosecutor and falsely convicted. The story of Tom Thompson, executed in 1998, shows the horrifying extent to which the AEDPA can be used to thwart justice.

Tom Thompson was sentenced to death in 1983 for the stabbing and alleged rape of a young woman in Laguna Beach, California. There was no physical evidence linking him to any crime. Due to the inaction of incompetent counsel, Thompson was convicted largely by the perjured testimony of two notoriously untruthful jailhouse informants, one of whom was released from parole in return for testifying. The prosecutor also took advantage of the fact that Thompson's semen—the result of consensual sex he had with the victim a few hours before she was killed—was found on her body. The prosecutor put forth a claim of rape even though there was no anatomical evidence to that effect, and illegally withheld Thompson's housemate's statement that he walked in on Thompson and Ginger Fleischli having consensual sex. The prosecutor claimed that Thompson—a man with no prior arrests or history of violence—murdered Ginger to conceal his rape.

There were numerous pieces of clear, physical evidence linking his housemate David Leitch, a man with a history of violence towards women, to the murder and the disposal of the body. Tom fell asleep after sex, and arrangements had been made earlier that Leitch would take Ginger home. There was also a motive. Leitch had been living with Ginger before Thompson moved into the apartment, but had thrown her out and threatened to kill her. He had been involved in a romantic triangle with Ginger and his ex-wife, and Ginger was trying to prevent Leitch's reconciliation with his ex-wife, who was Ginger's best friend.

The truth was not the concern of the prosecutor, Orange County Deputy D.A. Mike Jacobs, who took this opportunity to score a double victory and add two more convictions to his record instead of one. Jacobs convicted Thompson and Leitch in two separate trials, each as the killer, based on two different and conflicting scenarios that were presented to different juries. In fact, in Leitch's trial which followed Thompson's, the prosecutor made a strong argument that Thompson had no motive, and ridiculed the version of events he had presented at Thompson's trial. As to whether Thompson was the killer, Jacobs told the court "No, it didn't happen that way." In short, he told the court that Thompson didn't commit the acts for which he was already convicted by Jacobs and sentenced to death. Leitch was given a prison term, but Thompson was sentenced to death because of the accusation of rape.

The contradictory trials were so blatantly unethical that seven highly respected former California prosecutors with extensive death penalty experience—including the drafter of the California death penalty statute—filed an unprecedented brief in the U.S. Supreme Court. In criticism of the "egregious conduct" of Mike Jacobs, the group of top prosecutors pointed out "how easy it is to manipulate facts when the prosecutor's goal is to win at all costs."

Thompson's case took many steps and was dealt its final blow through the AEDPA. The Central District Court of California ruled in the first habeas corpus petition that the death sentence should be set aside due to incompetent lawyering and lack of evidence on the rape charge. The Ninth Circuit Court of Appeals, a higher federal court, agreed with the first habeas corpus ruling, reversing the rape conviction and vacating the death penalty. It established that the prosecutor violated due process. This ruling came about only hours before Thompson was scheduled to be executed in August 1997.

Yet the State appealed. In April 1998, the U.S. Supreme Court in a five to four decision then turned around and revoked this decision in the name of "finality." Now, enter the AEDPA. It wasn't until 1997 that the attorneys had discovered that the prosecution withheld the evidence of consensual sex from the defense. This almost certainly would have spared Thompson the death penalty, and would likely have also refuted the prosecutor's contrived theory that he was the murderer.

In the wake of the devastating decision from the Supreme Court, Thompson's attorneys moved quickly on the dramatic evidence of consensual sex. They filed a second habeas corpus petition in 1998 with the Ninth Circuit Court of Appeals. They requested a chance to develop this evidence and bring it into a hearing. This time, the same court that ruled earlier that the death sentence was erroneous had to deal with the new burden of the AEDPA. As a result of its restrictions, Thompson's motion was voted down—even though the new evidence had been deliberately concealed by state prosecutors in violation of the law—because the new evidence could not prove actual innocence.

This final petition was simply requesting the necessary judicial help to develop the powerful new evidence—such as a discovery order and an evidentiary hearing where prosecutors would be questioned under oath—so that the evidence could be presented to show actual innocence. But without these judicial tools, the evidence could not be brought to that standard. In a situation reminiscent of Shaka Sankofa's case, the AEDPA required that a full blown showing of "clear and convincing" evidence of innocence be presented up front. In reality, Thompson was never given a chance because the AEDPA asked for the impossible: proof of innocence without the necessary tools to present just that.

Since the court would not grant a new hearing, it prevented the truth from ever being heard by a jury. Tom Thompson was executed three days after the decision was issued, on July 14, 1998. "To those who are responsible for my false imprisonment: you can systematically torture me for seventeen years, you can even kill me, but you cannot change the fact that I am factually innocent," Thompson wrote in his final statement released the day before his execution.

Judge Stephen Reinhardt, an eighteen-year circuit judge for the United States Court of Appeals for the Ninth Circuit, was one of two judges who defied the AEDPA and voted against the final decision which sent Thompson to his death. He is convinced that Thompson "was not eligible for a death sentence." In a paper to be published in the *New York University Law Journal*, Reinhardt says that Thompson is "the first person in the nation ever to be executed on the basis of a trial that an unrefuted decision of a United States Court of Appeals had held to be unconstitutional."

Judge Reinhardt also writes that "the Thompson execution has ramifications that go far beyond the particular act of judicial disregard for fairness and justice that led to an execution that should never have occurred." His further reflection sums up the profound implications of the AEDPA. "When the state is out to execute the accused at all costs and the nation's highest court's primary interest is in establishing procedural rules that preclude federal courts from considering even the most egregious violations of a defendant's constitutional rights, it is time to step back and look at what we are doing to ourselves and to our system of justice."

Appellate attorney Rita Barker became very close to Tom Thompson during the last years of his life. She met him while doing some minor work on the case for one of Thompson's lead attorneys. "Tom was an innocent man," she said in a recent interview from her Sacramento law office. He was a Vietnam era veteran, very intelligent and informed about the legal issues. "Tom believed very much in this country, and that's why he enlisted and went to serve his country during the Vietnam War," says Barker. "He believed in the system all the way through. He always believed the system would do the right thing, and he would get his freedom back." She says that he was "astounded" at the AEDPA's final judgment. "The courts changed the rules on me," he said. Up until that final moment, he still had faith that justice would eventually be done.

One can only speculate what Thompson thought about the astounding fact that the AEDPA actually protected prosecutorial misconduct—which was in violation of the law—and instead executed the man whose sentence of death depended on this illegal act. This is "outrageous," says Barker. "The prosecutors were actually able to benefit from the illegal act of withholding evidence. They managed to keep it hidden all those years until the AEDPA was passed." The prosecutors were then able to protect their wrongdoings through the AEDPA, and have not been held accountable.

Rita Barker said her final goodbye to Thompson, whom she loved deeply, six hours before he was killed by lethal injection. "I apologized to him for the way his country had betrayed him and let him down," she says, moved to tears as she tells the story. "He told me that his conscience was clear. That the only concern he had was that his death would be in vain. And that he hoped that somehow it would make a difference and not be in vain. And I promised him that I would spend the rest of my life speaking the truth and trying to make the system acknowledge what it did to him."

A week after witnessing Tom's death, a heartbroken Barker wrote a letter to Judge Reinhardt expressing her gratitude for his opinions on the case which she said "shine as the voice of reason and moral truth." "I am still in shock that such an atrocity could happen in this country," she wrote. "I truly believe that one day this case will be recognized as the horrifying miscarriage of justice it truly is."

Eight months later, Rita Barker has a clear message for Henry Hyde, who bears a large portion of responsibility for the death of Thompson and the fate of many other Americans tried unjustly. "This evil legislation disembowels the writ of habeas corpus, which was installed by the framers of the Constitution to prevent just this sort of injustice. The legislation was passed for political gain. It is anti-American and it will continue to cause injustice. It is a heinous crime to pass such vicious legislation in the name of the victims of the Oklahoma City bombing. That's what I would like to say to Henry Hyde."

Courtesy of Rita Barker. Used by Permission.

Sucked into the black hole of Hyde's lethal legislation Tom Thompson with his friend Rita Barker on Valentine's Day, six months before he was executed. He was the first person in the country to be executed on the basis of a trial deemed unconstitutional by a U.S. Court of Appeals. Legislation sponsored and championed by Hyde protected illegal prosecutorial misconduct in Thompson's trial and led to the death of an innocent man.

> *"In closing, it is in my faith that my last act is that of forgiveness. I want it known that I forgive everybody who bore false witness against me. God bless Mike Jacobs. God bless you all, and take care."*

—Tom Thompson's final words in a written statement
to the people of California, July 13, 1998,
the day before his execution.

Index

A

abortion, 6–20, 28–29
  in cases of medical necessity, 18, 47–49
  in cases of rape and incest, 12, 18–20, 35
  censoring Internet communication about, 23–28
  Medicaid-funded, 8–10, 12, 15–19, 59. *see also* Hyde Amendment
  "partial-birth," 47–49
  in Third World, 20–23
abortion clinics, bombings of, 42–47
Abrams, Elliott, 148, 150, 152
ACLU. *see* American Civil Liberties Union
Administration Index (ADEX), 188
adultery. *see* Hancock, Cherie
Afghanistan, 117
Alan Guttmacher Institute, 15, 21, 23
Alvarez, Gustavo, 176
American Banker, 94
American Bar Association (ABA) Journal, 146
American Catholic Press, 41
American Civil Liberties Union (ACLU), 19, 25–27, 67
American Public Health Association, 10
Americas Watch, 129
Amnesty International's Piers Bannister, 201
Anderson, Tim, 78, 79, 81, 82, 85, 87, 95–99, 102, 104–108
Andrews Bell, Joan, 32, 34
Angelina, 18

Angola, 117
anti-communism, 143. *see also* Contras
Anti-Terrorism and Effective Death Penalty Act of April 1996 (AEDPA), 201–212, 218, 220–223
Aransas Princess luxury condominium, 84–86
Arguado, Marcos, 176
Arias, Oscar, 172
Arkansas S&L, 84–85, 97. *see also* Savings and Loan
The Austin American-Statesman, 188

B

Baker, Thurbert E., 206
Ballesteros, Ramon Matta, 160
banking. *see* House Banking; Savings and Loan
Barger, Brian, 180
Barker, Rita, 223–224
Barrett, John Q., 136
The Beast Reawakens (Lee, M.), 127
Berke, Alex, 61
Bermingham, Robert A., 158, 160–163, 165–167, 169, 175, 177
Big White Lie (Levine, M.), 171
Bloodsport, 86
Blum, Jack, 157, 162
Blumenthal, Sidney, 67
Boland Amendments, 116–119, 123, 139, 140, 142–144, 174
Bond Buyer, 81
Boren, David, 185
Bosnia, 194–196
Boston Globe, 9, 167
Bradlee, Ben, Jr., 187

Index

Brandley, Clarence, 210
Brejcha, Tom, 38
Brigade 2506, 168
Brinkerhoff, John, 184, 187
Britell, Maureen, 44–45, 47–49
Brody, Reed, 129–131
Brooks, Jack, 184–185
Buckwalter, Ronald, 27
Bueso Rosa, José, 176–177
Burden of Proof (CNN), 67
Burr, Richard, 198, 201–203
Burt, John, 32
Bush, George, 94, 96, 100,
   147–149, 151, 154, 156, 174,
   175, 179
   Iran-Contra pardons, 144–153
Bush Administration, 147, 150
Byrd, Robert, 88

C

Caballero, Alfredo, 160
Cable Splicer, 183, 187–189
Cagney, Jimmy, 136
Califano, Joseph, 68, 69
California, 15
California Specialized Training
   Institute (CSTI), 183
capital punishment, 198–224
   of innocent persons, 198–201,
   206–211
Carlton, Floyd, 160
Carter, Jimmy, 68
Carter, Rubin "Hurricane,"
   215–216
Casey, William, 117, 136
Castillo, Celerino, III, 172–173,
   176
Catholic Church, 125–126, 128
Catholics Against Capital
   Punishment (CACP), 205
Cayman Islands, 117
Cedarholm, Fred, 99–101

censorship of Internet, 23–28
Center for Constitutional Rights,
   123
Center for Disease Control (CDC),
   8, 10
Center for Reproductive Law and
   Policy (CRLP), 27
Central Intelligence Agency (CIA),
   3, 115–118, 125–127, 157, 158,
   160–162, 171–176, 178–181
Cesar, Octaviano, 163
Chamorro, Edgar, 117
Chanes, Francisco, 160
Chenoweth, Helen, 216
The Chicago Sun Times, 101
The Chicago Tribune, 46, 72, 106,
   108, 112, 113, 207
CIA. *see* Central Intelligence
   Agency
Circuit Court of Appeals. *see* Court
   of Appeals
"The Civil/Military Alliance in
   Emergency Management," 190
Civil Security Division of FEMA,
   183
Claridge, Dewey, 172
Clarridge, Duane Robert, 148, 152
Classified Information Procedures
   Act (CIPA), 154
Clayton, Fay, 33–34, 36, 40
Clines, Thomas G., 152
Clinton, Hillary, 31, 86, 87
Clinton, President William, 1, 2,
   14, 26, 28, 31, 34, 53, 61, 68,
   72, 95, 106, 124, 146, 147, 183,
   193, 194, 218. *see also* Lewinsky;
   Starr
   impeachment hearings and trial,
      114–115, 124, 132
   Monicagate, 137–141, 144
   sex life and affairs, 54, 64

Closed: 99 Ways to Stop Abortion
(Scheidler, J.), 29, 38

Clyde Chief Executive Officer, 79

Clyde Federal Savings and Loan
Association, 72, 74–79, 87, 95,
108. see also Savings and Loan
Board of Directors, 74, 79, 80,
87

Clyde National, 84

cocaine. see Contra drug investigation

Cocaine Politics: Drugs, Armies, and
the CIA in Central America
(Scott, P.D. & Marshall, J.),
165, 166

Coffey, Alan, 26

Cohen, William, 133, 138–139, 141

Collins, Cardiss, 13

Colombia, 161, 162, 168

Commission on Human Rights, 211

communism. see anti-communism;
Sandinistas

Comstock law, 24

Conference of Community and
Justice, 55

Congress, 204

Congressional Accountability
Project (CAP), 78–79, 81, 82,
90, 106, 109, 112

Connor, Kathy, 35–36

Constitution, U.S., 4, 182–185,
187, 191, 195, 201, 212, 216

constitutional crises, 120–124,
132–133, 191, 204. see also capital punishment

Contra drug investigation, 2,
156–181, 189. see also Contras

Contra Terror in Nicaragua, 129–130

Contras, 3–4, 116, 117, 127–133,
136, 143, 151–153. see also Iran-
Contra affair

Hyde as "bomb thrower" for the,
124–128

Conyers, John, 24, 217

Cordova, Roberto Suazo, 176

Costa Rica, 164, 165, 168, 172, 173,
176

Costa Rica Justice Department, 172

Cotton, Richard, 70

Court of Appeals, 77, 203, 220–222

Cox, Christopher, 213

Crane, Dan, 68–71

Crane's Business News Service, 103

Cranes Business Weekly, 102

Croatia, 194–196

Cruz, Rolando, 208

Cuba, 187

Cunningham, Mirna, 131

Cusack, John T., 167

D

Daily Oklahoman, 13

Dallas Morning News, 54

Darrow, Clarence, 1

Dateline NBC, 18

DEA. see Drug Enforcement
Agency

death penalty. see capital punishment

Death Penalty Information Center,
210, 217

Defense Department, 188, 190

DeGette, Diana, 14

Delaware Women's Health
Organization, 35

DeMoss, Judge, 204

Deputy for National Preparedness
Programs, 184

Derwinski, Edwin, 96, 98

DIACSA, 160

District Court, 81

Dole, Bob, 213

Index

Drug Enforcement Agency (DEA), 157, 163, 171–173, 175
drugs. *see* Contra drug investigation
Duff, Brian Barnett, 77
DuPage County, 208

E

El Salvador, 163, 169, 172–173
Ethics Committee. *see* House Ethics Committee
Ethics in Government Act, 140
Eureka Federal Savings, 84
Evangelina, 7

F

family planning funding for Third World, 20–23
FBI. *see* Federal Bureau of Investigation
FCC. *see* Federal Communications Commissions
FDIC, 73, 80, 88, 90, 92
FDIC/Clyde settlement, 101
Federal Bureau of Investigation (FBI), 2, 66–68, 164–165, 176, 188, 217
Federal Communications Commissions (FCC), 26
Federal Deposit Insurance Corporation. *see* FDIC
Federal Emergency Management Agency (FEMA), 183, 184, 186, 188–191
Civil Security Division, 191
Federal Home Loan Bank Board, 78, 80
Federal Regulatory Agencies, 76
Federal Reserve Bank of Cleveland, 89
FEMA. *see* Federal Emergency Management Agency
Femcare, 3

Fernandez, Joseph F., 154, 172, 180
Fiers, Alan D., Jr., 148, 152, 161
Fiscal Year 1997 Omnibus Appropriations Bill, 14
Fisher, Zachary, 103
Fleischli, Ginger, 219
Fooling America: How Washington Insiders Twist the Truth and Manufacture Conventional Wisdom (Parry, R.), 125–126
Forbes, 82
Forman, Fred, 98
Foster, Vince, 86
Frankfurt, Ellen, 8–11
free speech. *see* censorship of Internet
Freedom of Access to Clinic Entrances Act (FACE), 33
Freedom of Information Act, 77, 105
Freeh, Louis J., 67
Fricker, Mary, 84
Friedersdorf, Max L., 122
Frigorificos de Puntarenas, 160
"Frogman Case," 168
The Futures Group, 21

G

Gacy, John Wayne, 217
Galbraith, Peter, 194, 196, 197
Gardner, Norman H., Jr., 142
Garn St. Germain legislation, 73, 76
George, Claire E., 148, 152, 180
Gesell, Gerhard, 153
Gingrich, Newt, 69, 194
Giuffrida, Louis O., 183, 187, 190
Gomez, Max. *see* Rodriguez, Felix
Gonzalez, Julia Picado, 130, 188
Gore, Al, 26
Government Accountability Office, 101

Graham, Dennis, 199
Graham, Gary. see Sankofa, Shaka
Grand Cayman Certificates of
    Deposit (CDs), 82, 83
Grand Cayman Islands bank, 82, 83
Gratiam Dei award, 41
Greene, Harold, 153
Gross, Norman, 57
Guaranty Savings and Loan
    Association, 84, 86, 87
Guevara, Che, 174
Guirola Beeche, Francisco, 173–174

H

Haines, Donald, 25
Hakim, Albert, 153
Hamilton, Lee, 158
Hancock, Cherie (ex-lover), 50–52,
    54–66, 71
Harrison, Moses, II, 208
Hasenfus, Eugene, 161, 175
Henry J. Hyde Defense Fund Trust,
    102, 103
hero worship, 34–41
Hill, Susan, 35–37, 39
Hilton, Claude, 154
Hitler, Adolf, 31
Honduras, 116, 131, 176, 188
Hopkins, Elaine, 97
Hopkins & Sutter, 102
House Banking, 79
House Banking Committee, 76, 80,
    82, 83
House Ethics Committee, 68, 69,
    72, 106, 109
House Intelligence Committee, 158
House International Relations
    Committee, 194–195
House Judiciary Committee. see
    Judiciary Committee

House of Representatives, 1, 2, 20,
    24, 28, 69, 194, 201. see also
    Congress
House Select Committee, 141
House Select Committee on
    Narcotics Abuse and Control,
    166
House Subcommittee on Western
    Hemisphere Affairs, 169, 170
Hubel, Wes, 86
Hull, John, 164, 165, 172
Hyde, Henry J. see also specific topics
    adultery. see Hancock, Cherie
    as "bomb thrower" for the
        Contras, 124–128
    as House Judiciary Chairman,
        72, 83, 86
    legacy, 1–5
Hyde, Jeanne, 62, 64, 65
Hyde Amendment, 5, 8, 10–16, 19,
    27, 31, 59, 210. see also abortion
"Hyde's Corollary," 150–151
hypocrisy, 50–60

I

Illinois Legal Times, 86
Illinois S&L. see Savings and Loan
    (S&L)
Ilopango, 172, 175, 176
immunity, granting, 133–134
impeachment hearings and trial. see
    under Clinton
Inouye, Daniel, 184–185
*Inside Job: The Looting of America's
    Savings and Loans*, 84
Institute on Religion and
    Democracy (IRD), 127
Intelligence Committee
    House, 158
    Senate, 157
Intelligence Oversight Board, 118
Internet, censorship of, 23–28

Index

intimidation, 66–68
Iran, 152
Iran-Contra affair, 115, 121–123,
    126, 132, 137, 142, 144–148,
    180–182, 193, 195. see also
    Contras
    Monicagate vs., 137–141
Iran-Contra committees, 119, 135,
    140, 141, 156, 158, 175
Iran-Contra hearings, 149, 150, 174
Iran-Contra pardons, 144–153
The Iran-Contra Scandal, 122

J

Jacobs, Mike, 219–220
James, Jesse, 73
Jiminez, Rosie, 6–11, 22
Jolly, Judge, 204
Journal Star, 97
Judiciary Committee, 23, 24, 26, 37,
    39, 47, 53, 72, 79, 83, 86, 87,
    90, 91, 95, 101–103, 105, 146,
    211, 216
Justice Department
    Costa Rica, 172
    U.S., 3, 25, 66, 161, 162, 177,
        186, 197

K

Kane, Ed, 93–95
Karkula, Paul A., 112
Kendall, David, 105, 106
Kendall, George, 202, 209, 211
Kerry, John, 157, 161–163, 169, 171
Khomeini, Ayatollah, 151
King, Judge, 204
Kissling, Frances, 8–11
Kiszynski, George, 164
Knight, Robert, 167
Koppel, Ted, 31
Kornbluh, Peter, 115, 122, 143

L

Labat Anderson, 103
Lake, Anthony, 197
Lake Resources Inc., 153
Lambert, Bobby, 198
League of Savings Institutions,
    U.S., 96, 100
Lee, Martin, 127
LeGrand, Ronald A., 167
Leitch, David, 219, 220
Levine, Michael, 157, 158, 171, 172
Lewinsky, Monica, 64, 72. see also
    Monicagate
Liman, Arthur, 185
Lincoln, Abraham, 1
Los Angeles Times, 94, 194
lying about sex, 63–65, 70–71
Lyons, Emily, 3, 42, 44–47

M

Madigan, Edward, 96, 98
Mafia, 175
Malinowski, Walter, 103
Marsh, Jeremiah, 102, 103
Marshall, Jonathan, 165, 166, 169
martial law, 189–192
McAllen, 8
McBirney, Ed, 73
McCollum, Bill, 124
McCurry, Mike, 67
McFarlane, Robert, 122, 124, 125,
    142, 147, 186, 188
McGill, Catherine, 14–18, 20
McGrory, Mary, 135
McKinney, Cynthia A., 12–13
McNeil-Lehrer News Hour, 147
McNeirney, Frank, 205, 206
Medellin Cartel, 160, 162, 176,
    178, 181
Medicaid funding for abortion,
    8–10, 12, 15–19, 59
Meese, Edwin, 136, 183, 187, 188

Men of Zeal: A Candid Story of the Iran-Contra Affair (Cohen, W. & Mitchell, G.), 138–139

Mexico, 9, 10

Miami Herald, 182, 184–187, 190

Miami Metropolitan Correctional Center, 164

Miedema, Sylvia, 74, 79

Miller, Robert, 214

Miriam, 57

Mitchell, George, 138–139

Mock, Ron, 198

Monicagate, 137–141, 144. *see also* Clinton; Lewinsky, Monica

Morales, George, 163–165

Moynihan, Daniel Patrick, 201

Muolo, Paul, 84

Murphy, Laura W., 25

N

Nader, Ralph, 81, 91, 92

NAF. *see* National Abortion Federation

National Abortion and Reproductive Rights Action League (NARAL), 27

National Abortion Federation (NAF), 14, 17–19, 42, 44

National Association for the Advancement of Colored People (NAACP) Legal Defense Fund, 202

National Association of Securities Dealers (NASD), 81–82

National Commission on Financial Institution Reform, Recovery and Enforcement, 97

National Guard, 188

National Law Journal, 100, 132

National Organization for Women (NOW), 32, 33, 38

National Security Archives, 115

National Security Council (NSC), 116–118, 136, 139, 140, 142, 143, 157, 160, 183, 184, 186, 188. *see also* McFarlane

National Security Decision Directive 52, 187–188

National Women's Health Organization, 37

Native Americans, 12

Ndiaye, Bacre Waly, 211

New Republic, 94, 139

New York, 15

The New York Times, 9, 90, 94

New York University Law Journal, 222

News Talk 89, 110

Newsday, 167–169

Newsweek, 125

Nicaragua, 116, 132, 138, 150–151, 170, 187, 190. *see also* Contras; Sandinistas

Nicaraguan Democratic Forces (FDN), 127

Nicaraguan Democratic Union, 168

Nicaraguan Humanitarian Assistance Office (NHAO), 160, 161, 168–170

Nicaraguan Revolutionary Armed Force, 168

Nicaraguans in Exile, Conservative Party of, 168

Nields, John, 158

99 Ways to Stop Abortion (Scheidler, J.), 38

Noriega, Manuel, 176

North, Oliver L., 3, 71, 115, 117–121, 123, 125, 134–136, 138, 141, 143, 145, 146, 153, 156, 157, 160, 161, 169–173, 177–179, 181–187, 189–191

Under Fire: An American Story, 140

Index

immunity granted to, 133–134, 153–155

NSC. *see* National Security Council

O

Obando y Bravo, Cardinal, 125–128

O'Brien, Conor Cruise, 128

Ocean Hunter, 160

Ochoa, Jorge, 162

Oklahoma City bombing, 212–216, 224

Oldenburg, J. William, 83–88

Omnibus Appropriations Bill, 14

Operation Rescue, 29, 32

Ortiz, Maria Julia, 131

Owen, Rob, 161

P

Packaging the Contras: A Case of CIA Disinformation, 117–118

Palacio, Wanda, 161–162, 165

Palmer, Michael, 160, 161

Parry, Robert, 125, 126, 138, 180–181

Peace Corps volunteers, 12

Pentagon, 115, 118

Peoria-Journal Star, 51

perjury, 34. *see also* lying about sex

Philip, James "Pate," 207–208

Pineda, Maria, 7, 8

Piner, Martin, 131

Pitchford, Marla, 10

Pizzo, Stephen, 84

Poindexter, John M., 116–117, 123, 134, 136, 141, 142, 145, 153, 172, 177

Pope, 59

Population Action International, 21

Population Council, 21

Population Reference Bureau, 21

Porter, Anthony, 207

Posada Carrilles, Luis, 175

poverty, 6, 11–14

Pro-Life Action League, 29, 31, 205

Pro-Life Action Network (PLAN), 28–30, 32

Pugh, Tom, 51

R

Racketeer Influenced and Corrupt Organizations (RICO) Act, 32–33, 40, 42, 43, 46–47

Raleigh Women's Health Organization, 39

Ramsey, Thomas, 152

Rangel, Charles, 165–169

Rangel Committee, 167

rape. *see* abortion, in cases of rape

Ratner, Michael, 123, 142

Reagan, Ronald, 74, 118, 126, 136, 141–143, 145, 146, 149, 156, 157, 182, 183, 186, 187, 189, 190

Reagan administration, 121, 123, 126, 128, 147–150, 181, 182, 190, 193. *see also specific individuals*

Refco, 87

Reinhardt, Stephen, 222

Religious Freedom Award, 127

Reno, Janet, 26

Republican Policy Committee, 86

Resolution Trust Corporation of America (RTC), 76, 77, 80, 87, 98–100

Rex-84 Bravo, 187–188

Reynolds, Diana, 189–191

RICO Act. *see* Racketeer Influenced and Corrupt Organizations Act

Rizzo, Ernie, 105–113

Robinson, Aubrey, 152

Rockefeller Foundation, 21–22

Rodriguez, Felix, 173–176
Roe *vs.* Wade, 27
Roll Call, 68, 109
Roman Catholic Church. *see*
    Catholic Church
Rose Law Firm, 86, 87
*Rosie: The Investigation of a Wrongful
    Death* (Frankfurt, F. and
    Kissling, F.), 8
Rudman, Warren, 119, 133, 185
Ruskin, Gary, 80, 90, 91, 98, 99

S

Sachnoff, Lowell, 37, 39
Salcedo, Frank S., 191
Salon, 52–54, 56, 63–66, 68
Salt Lake City S&L, 84
Saltzburg, Stephen, 137–138
San Antonio Express-News, 54
Sanderson, Robert, 47
Sandinista government, 116
Sandinistas, 125, 126, 128, 135,
    144, 151
Sankofa, Shaka, 198–201
Saporta, Vicky, 44, 46, 47
Sarah Scaife Foundation, 127
Saudi Arabia, 117
Savings and Loan (S&L), 2, 72–113
Sawyer, Wallace "Buzz," 161
Scheidler, Ann, 205
Scheidler, Joseph, 28–41, 44, 46,
    205
Schippers, David, 106
Schirott, James, 106–109, 112
Schlup, Lloyd, 210
Schroeder, Patricia, 23–28
Sciaroni, Bretton, 118–120, 139
Scott, Peter Dale, 165, 166, 169
Secord, Richard V., 153, 172
Securities and Exchange
    Commission (SEC), 81, 84

Select Committee on Narcotics,
    165, 166
Senate, 12, 70, 194, 195, 201. *see
    also* Congress
Senate Foreign Relations
    Subcommittee on Terrorism,
    Narcotics, and International
    Operations, 157
Senate Intelligence Committee,
    157
Senate Select Committee, 141
Senate Subcommittee on Terrorism,
    Narcotics, and International
    Communications, 162
Serbia, 194
SETCO Air, 160
Sevilla, Jamilet, 130
sexual affairs, 68–69. *see also*
    Clinton, sex life; Hancock,
    Cherie
    lying about, 63–65, 70–71
Simpson, OJ, 106
Skinner, Nancy, 110–112
S&L. *see* Savings and Loan
Slaughter, Louise, 22
Smeeton, Thomas, 103
Smith, Steven, 207–208
Smith, William French, 157, 186
Smith Richardson Foundation, 127
Snodgrass, Fred, 52, 54, 60–62, 64,
    66
Socrates, 1
Sommer, Norman, 52–53, 61,
    66–68
Southern Air Transport, 161
Starr, Kenneth, 68, 69, 72, 86, 87,
    105, 146
Starr report, 55
State Department, 160, 165, 169
    Office of Public Diplomacy, 190
State House, 62
Stephenson, Edward, 101

Index

Stevenson, Adlai, 50
Stewart, James, 86
Stratman, Sam, 108, 110, 111
Studs, Gerry, 70
Sullivan, Brendan, 140–141
Sullivan, Sean, 90
Supreme Court justices, 44
Supreme Court rulings, 27, 220, 221
Swink, Jimmy Dale, Sr., 81–83, 86–88
Swink & Co., 81, 82

T

Tambs, Lewis, 127
Tarnoff, Peter, 194–195
Telecom bill, 23, 25, 26
Teresa, Mother, 1, 6, 12
Terry, Randal, 29
Texas, 8–9, 16
The Washington Post, 9
The Washington Times, 181
Third World, funding for family planning and abortion in, 20–23
Thompson, Paul, 218–223
Thompson, Tom, 5, 218–220
Thornburgh, Dick, 154
Todd, Walker, 89
treason, 157–158. *see also* Contra drug investigation
"Truth Squad," 50, 51
Tudjman, Franjo, 194

U

Ubeda, Digna Barreda de, 130–131
Under Fire: An American Story (North, O.), 140
UNICEF, 22
United Nations, 194, 195, 211
United Nations Security Council, 195
United Nations Special Rapporteur, 211

USA Today, 1

V

van Sustern, Greta, 67
Vidal, Felipe, 160
Vortex, 160
Vrdolyak, Edward, 111–113

W

The Wall Street Journal, 84
Walsh, Lawrence, 117, 120, 121, 133, 134, 136, 145–148, 154–155, 179–180
Washington Post, 94, 165–166, 169, 181, 187
Watt, Melvin, 216
Webb, Dan K., 142
Webster, William, 179, 188
Weinberger, Caspar W., 145, 148–151
Weiner, Robert, 167
Welch, Bud, 213–216
Wheeler, Betty, 23, 25
White, Robert, 169
White House, 66–67, 100, 197. *see also specific presidents*
Whitewater, 86–87
Winer, Jonathan, 169
WLS (radio station), 110, 111

Z

Zavala, Julio, 168

About the Authors

DENNIS BERNSTEIN is an associate editor with the San Francisco-based Pacific News Service, and the host/producer of *Flashpoints*, a daily newsmagazine heard on Bay Area public radio. He is the recipient of many awards for his investigative reporting, including the Jessie Meriton White Service Award in International Journalism, the Art of Peace Award and the National Federation of Community Broadcasters Award. Project Censored, the national media watchdog group, has recognized Bernstein's investigative reporting more than a half-dozen times since 1990. Bernstein's articles and essays have appeared in numerous magazines, newspapers and journals around the world and in many anthologies.

LESLIE KEAN is a journalist and an associate producer/host for Pacifica Radio's *Flashpoints* on KPFA. Her articles with Dennis Bernstein have appeared in newspapers and magazines such as *The Nation*, the *Boston Globe*, the *Baltimore Sun*, the *International Herald Tribune*, the *San Francisco Examiner*, the *Sacramento Bee*, the *Globe and Mail*, the *Sydney Morning Herald*, the *Kyoto Journal* and *The Progressive*. She is the co-author of *Burma's Revolution of the Spirit: The Struggle for Democratic Freedom and Dignity* and the director of the Burma Project USA, a human rights and media advocacy group.